The
terrible and
wonderful
reasons why I

long distances

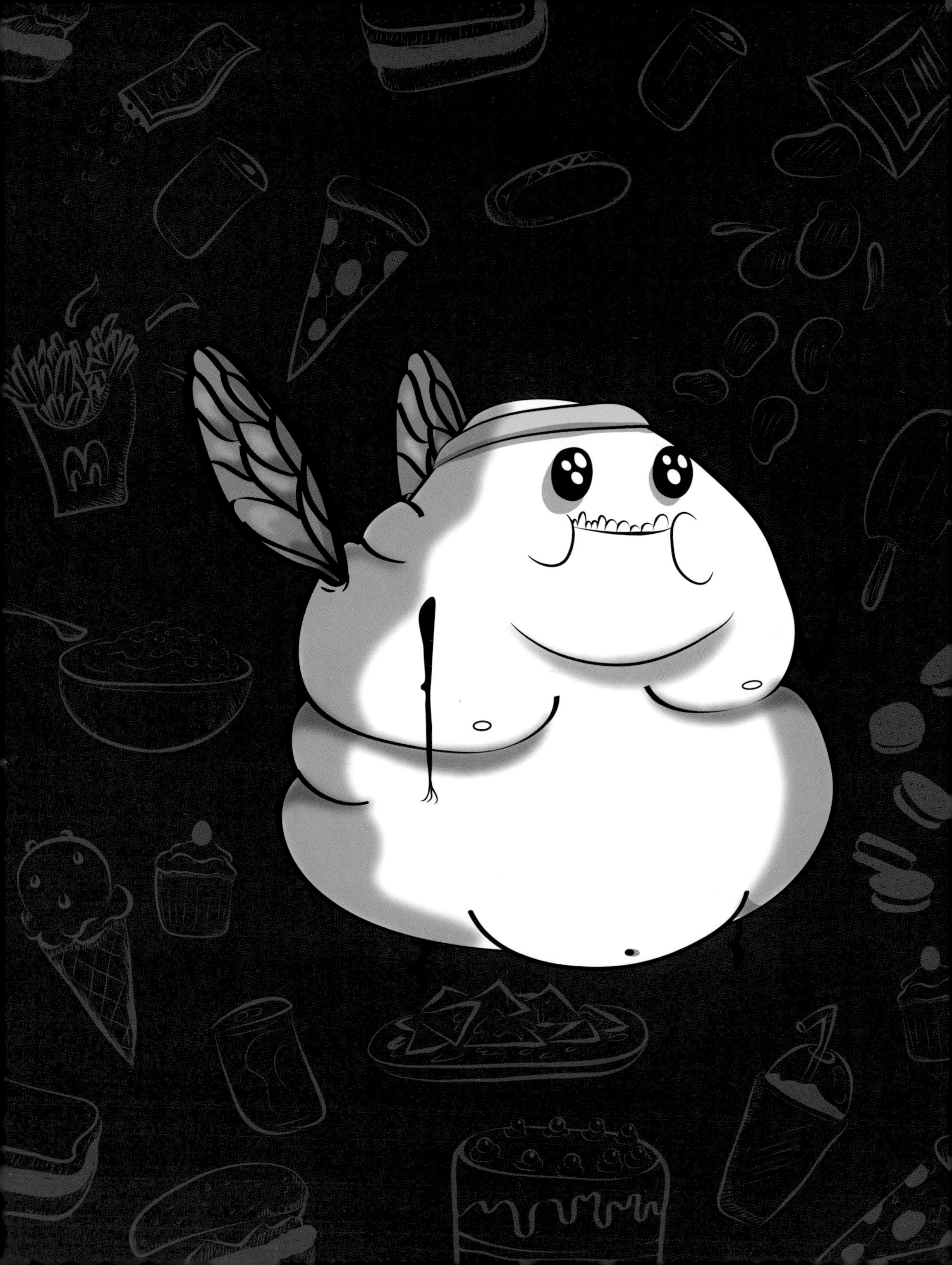

The terrible and **wonderful** reasons why I run long distances

Oatmeal

Andrews McMeel
Publishing

Kansas City • Sydney • London

Table of contents

The terrible and wonderful reasons why I run long distances

Nearly a decade ago,
I started running.

It began with short little jogs, and then I moved on to 5ks, 10ks, half marathons, full marathons, triathlons, and eventually

ultra marathons.

In 2011 I ran my first ultra, and it was a 50 mile mountain run with a total elevation change of 17,400 feet. My toenails fell off, I lost seven pounds in a day, and it took eleven hours.

For me, running has always been a meditative act; when I run, I think. Most of my comics are written in my head while running, so it suffices to say that running an eleven hour race in addition to the days, months, and years of training that preceded it afforded me plenty of time to take a hard, honest look at *why* I run. These thoughts ultimately culminated into this comic.

So without further ado, I present:

The
terrible & Wonderful
reasons why I
run long distances

Part 1. The Blerch

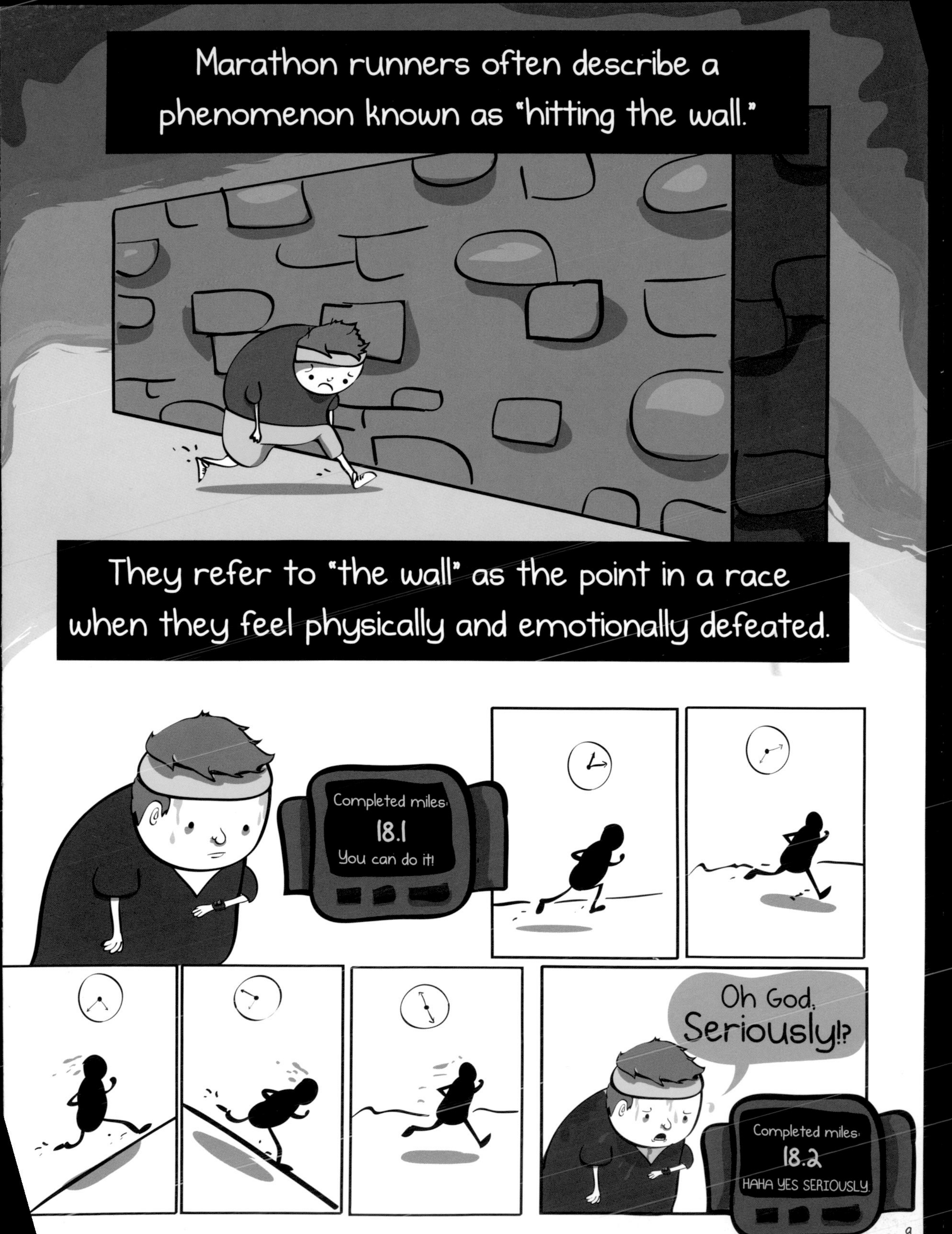
Marathon runners often describe a phenomenon known as "hitting the wall."
They refer to "the wall" as the point in a race when they feel physically and emotionally defeated.
Completed miles: 18.1 You can do it!
Oh God, Seriously!?
Completed miles: 18.2 HAHA YES SERIOUSLY.

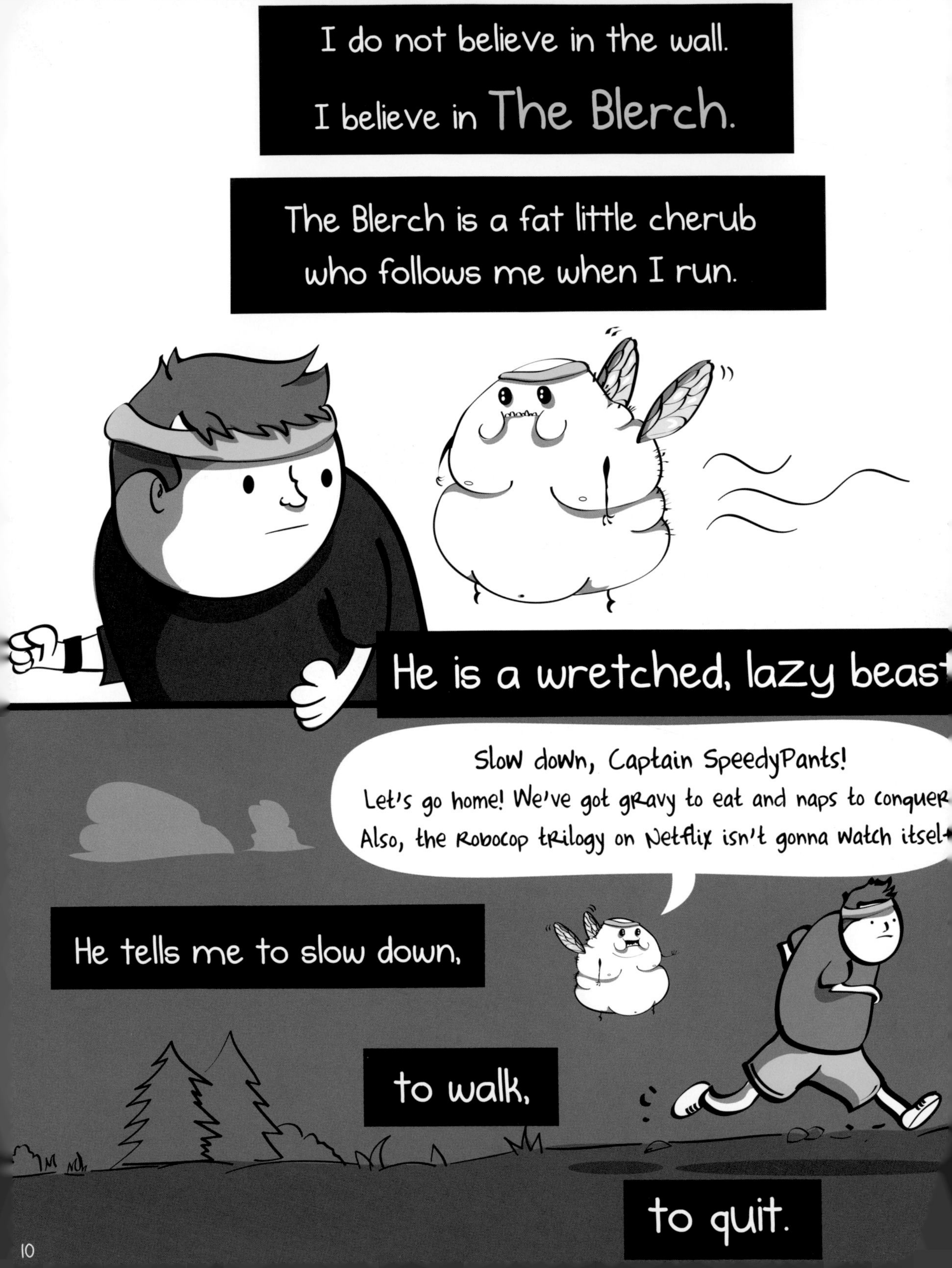
I do not believe in the wall.
I believe in The Blerch.
The Blerch is a fat little cherub who follows me when I run.
He is a wretched, lazy beast
Slow down, Captain SpeedyPants! Let's go home! We've got gravy to eat and naps to conquer Also, the Robocop trilogy on Netflix isn't gonna watch itsel
He tells me to slow down,
to walk,
to quit.

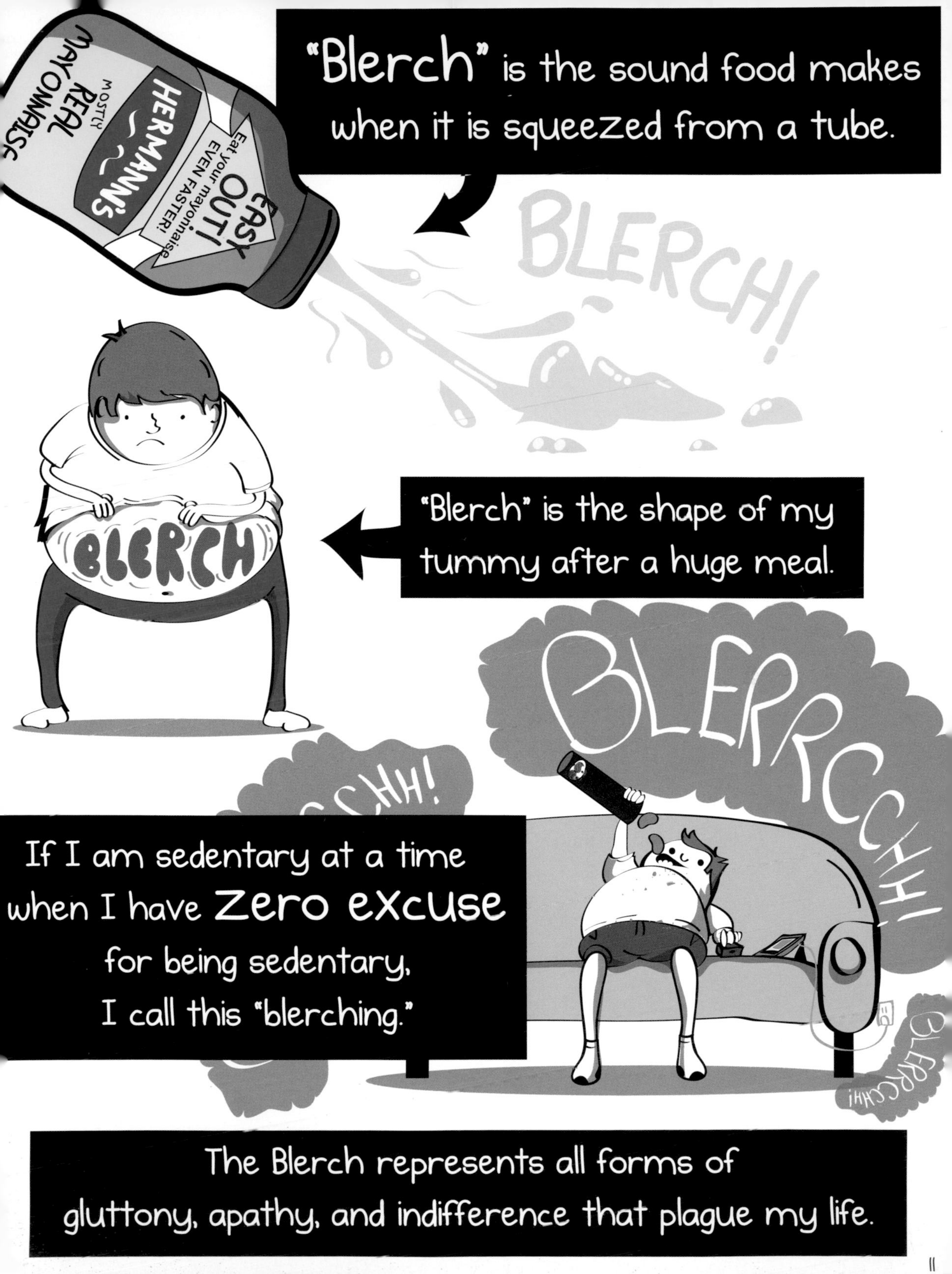

"Blerch" is the sound food makes when it is squeezed from a tube.
HERMANN'S
MOSTLY REAL MAYONNAISE
EASY OUT!
Eat your mayonnaise EVEN FASTER!
BLERCH!
"Blerch" is the shape of my tummy after a huge meal.
BLERCH
BLERRCCHH!
If I am sedentary at a time when I have zero excuse for being sedentary, I call this "blerching."
BLERRCHH!
The Blerch represents all forms of gluttony, apathy, and indifference that plague my life.

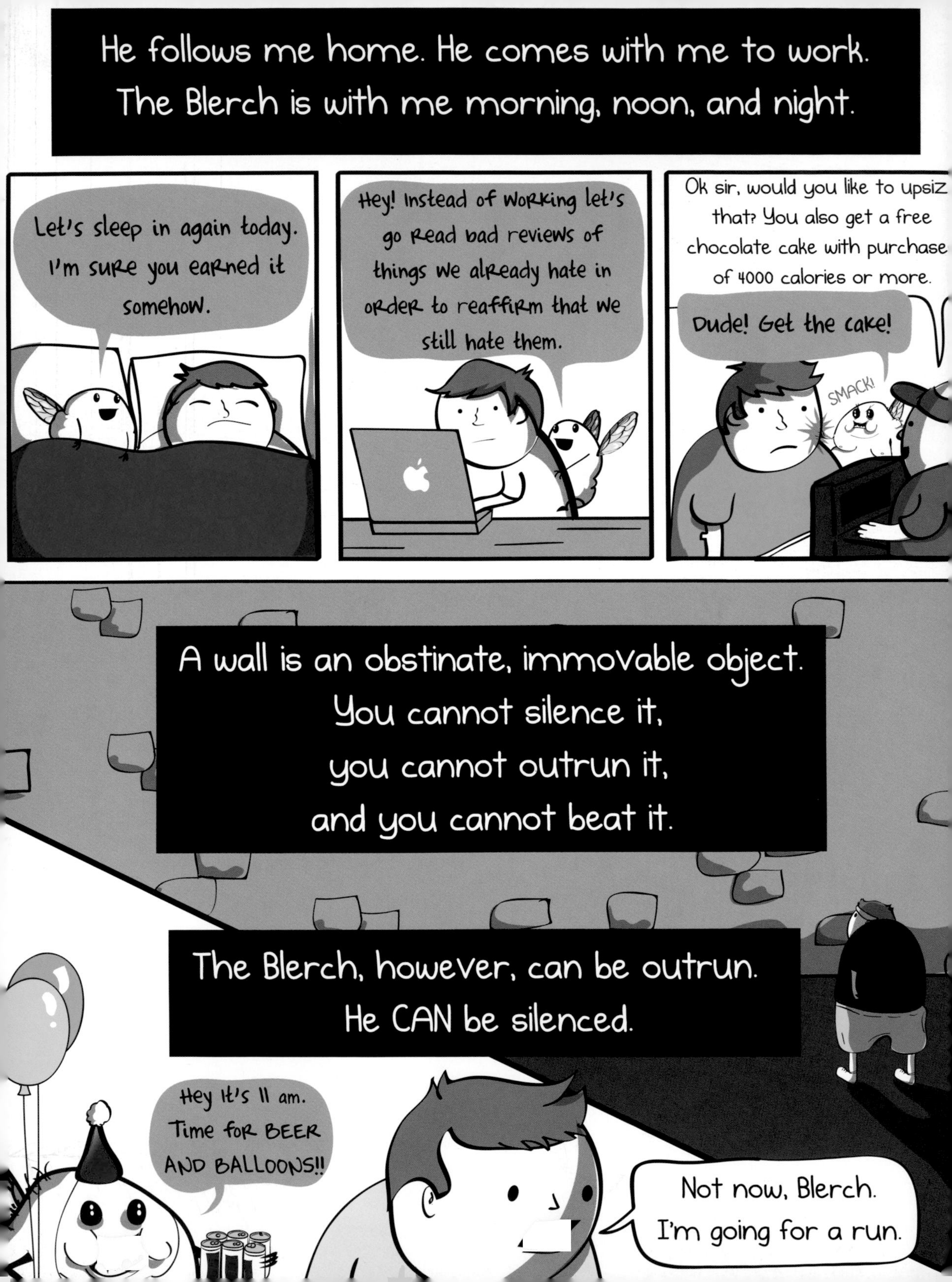
He follows me home. He comes with me to work.
The Blerch is with me morning, noon, and night.
Let's sleep in again today. I'm sure you earned it somehow.
Hey! Instead of working let's go read bad reviews of things we already hate in order to reaffirm that we still hate them.
Ok sir, would you like to upsiz that? You also get a free chocolate cake with purchase of 4000 calories or more.
Dude! Get the cake!
SMACK!
A wall is an obstinate, immovable object.
You cannot silence it,
you cannot outrun it,
and you cannot beat it.
The Blerch, however, can be outrun.
He CAN be silenced.
Hey it's 11 am. Time for BEER AND BALLOONS!!
Not now, Blerch. I'm going for a run.

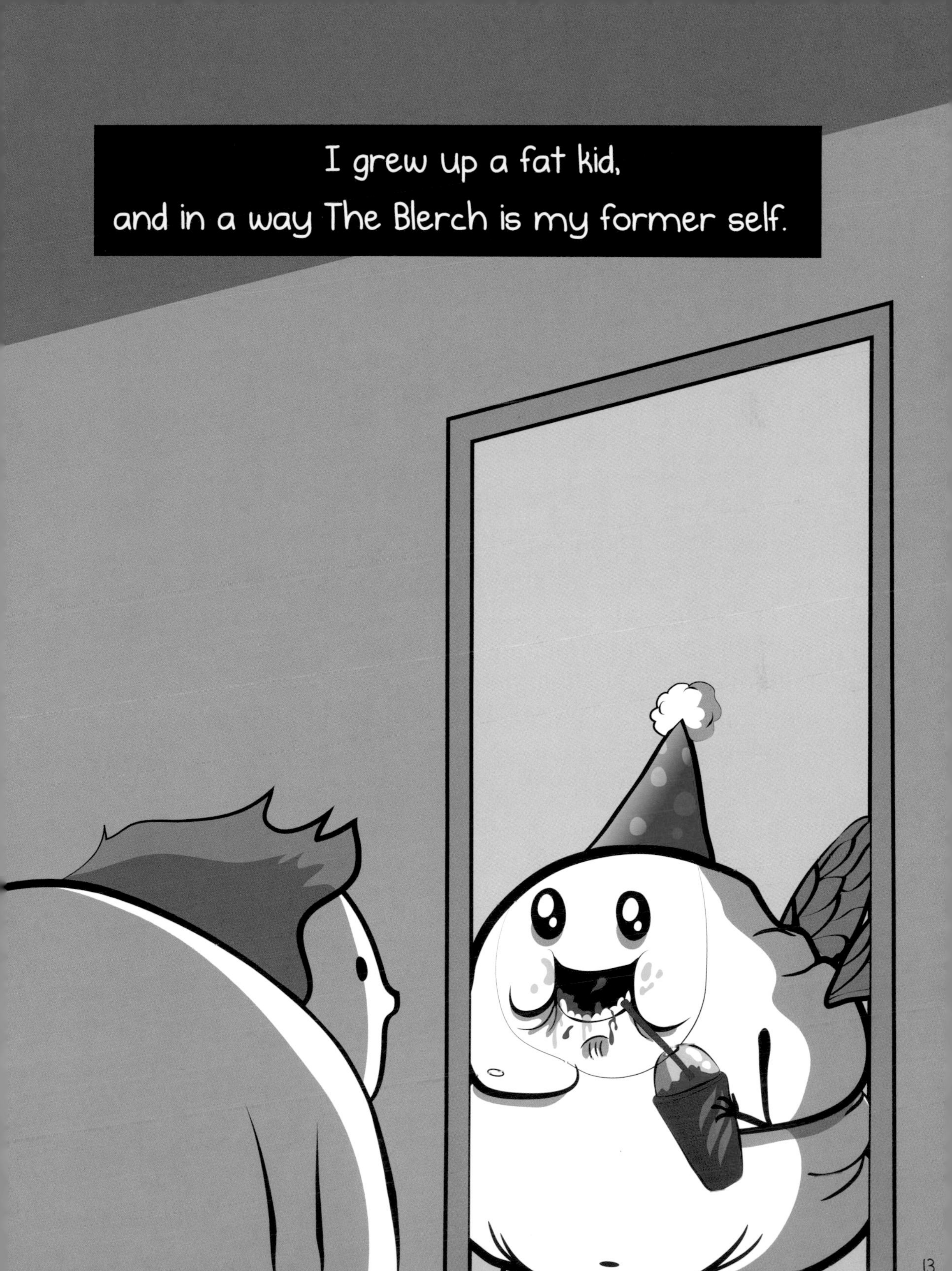
I grew up a fat kid,
and in a way The Blerch is my former self.

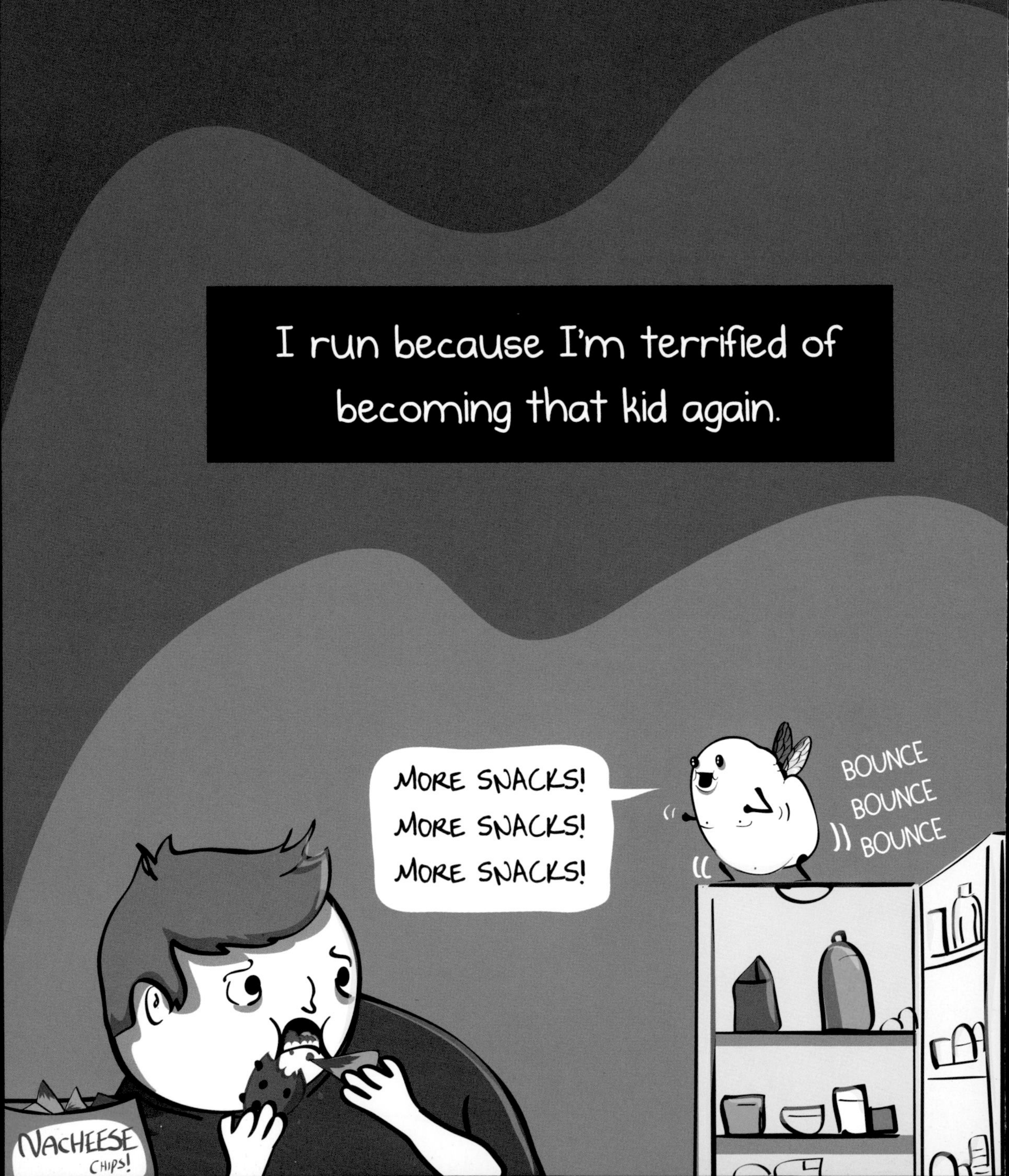
I run because I'm terrified of becoming that kid again.
MORE SNACKS! MORE SNACKS! MORE SNACKS!
BOUNCE BOUNCE BOUNCE
NACHEESE CHIPS!

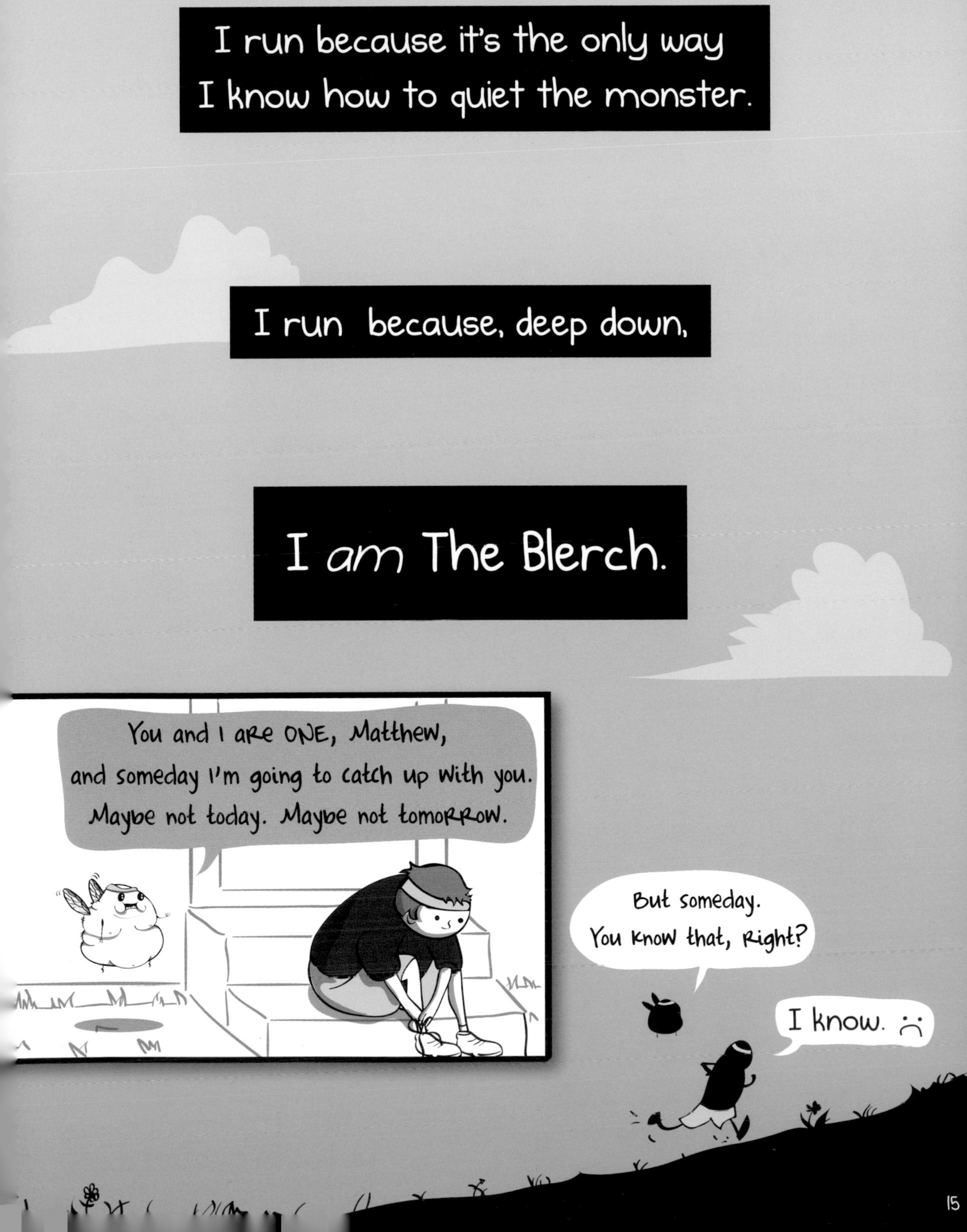
I run because it's the only way I know how to quiet the monster.
I run because, deep down,
I *am* The Blerch.
You and I aRe ONE, Matthew, and someday I'm going to catch up with you. Maybe not today. Maybe not tomoRRow.
But someday. You know that, Right?
I know. :(

Part 2. The ~~Eating~~ Feeding

There is a stereotype that if you're a runner, you're the type of person who celebrates ALL forms of healthy living.

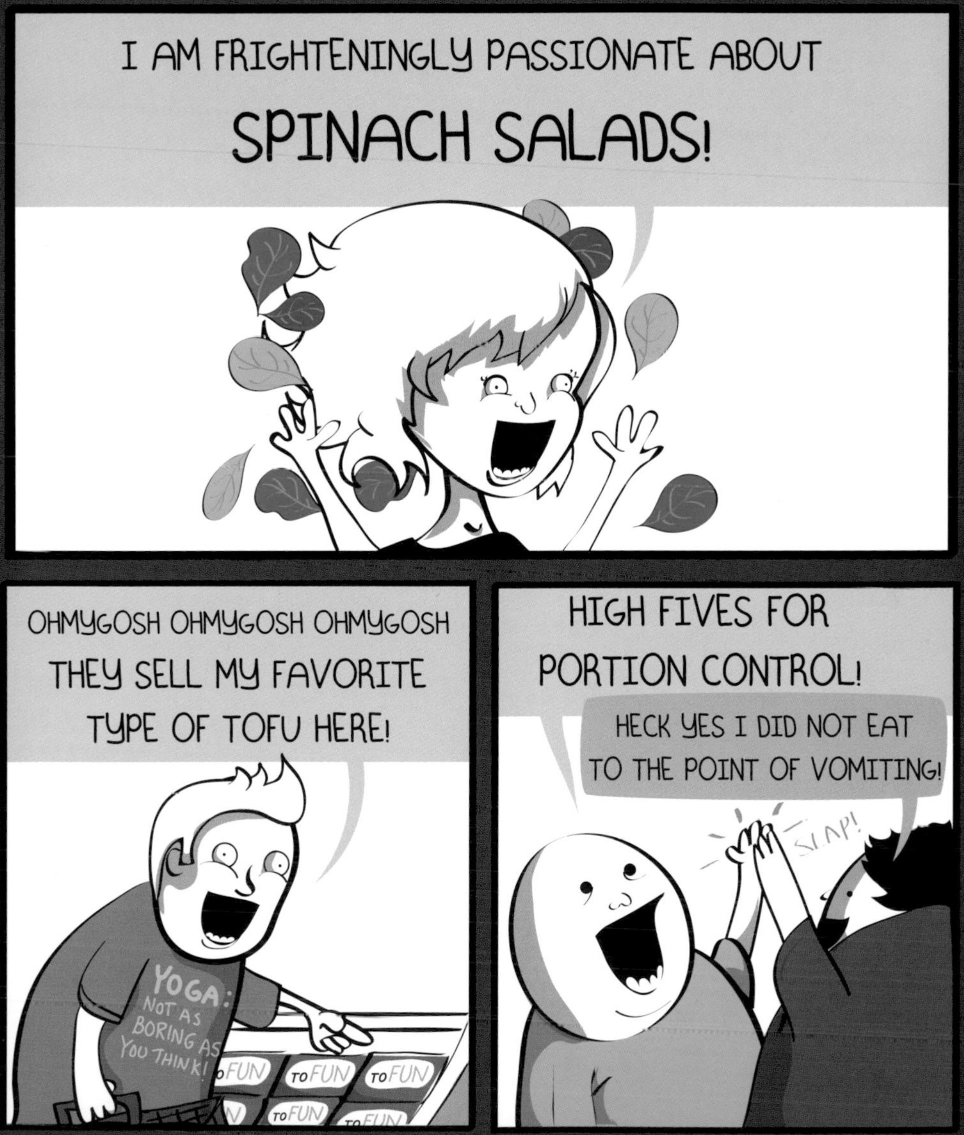
I AM FRIGHTENINGLY PASSIONATE ABOUT
SPINACH SALADS!
OHMYGOSH OHMYGOSH OHMYGOSH
THEY SELL MY FAVORITE TYPE OF TOFU HERE!
YOGA: NOT AS BORING AS YOU THINK!
TOFUN
HIGH FIVES FOR PORTION CONTROL!
HECK YES I DID NOT EAT TO THE POINT OF VOMITING!
SLAP!

I am not that type of person.

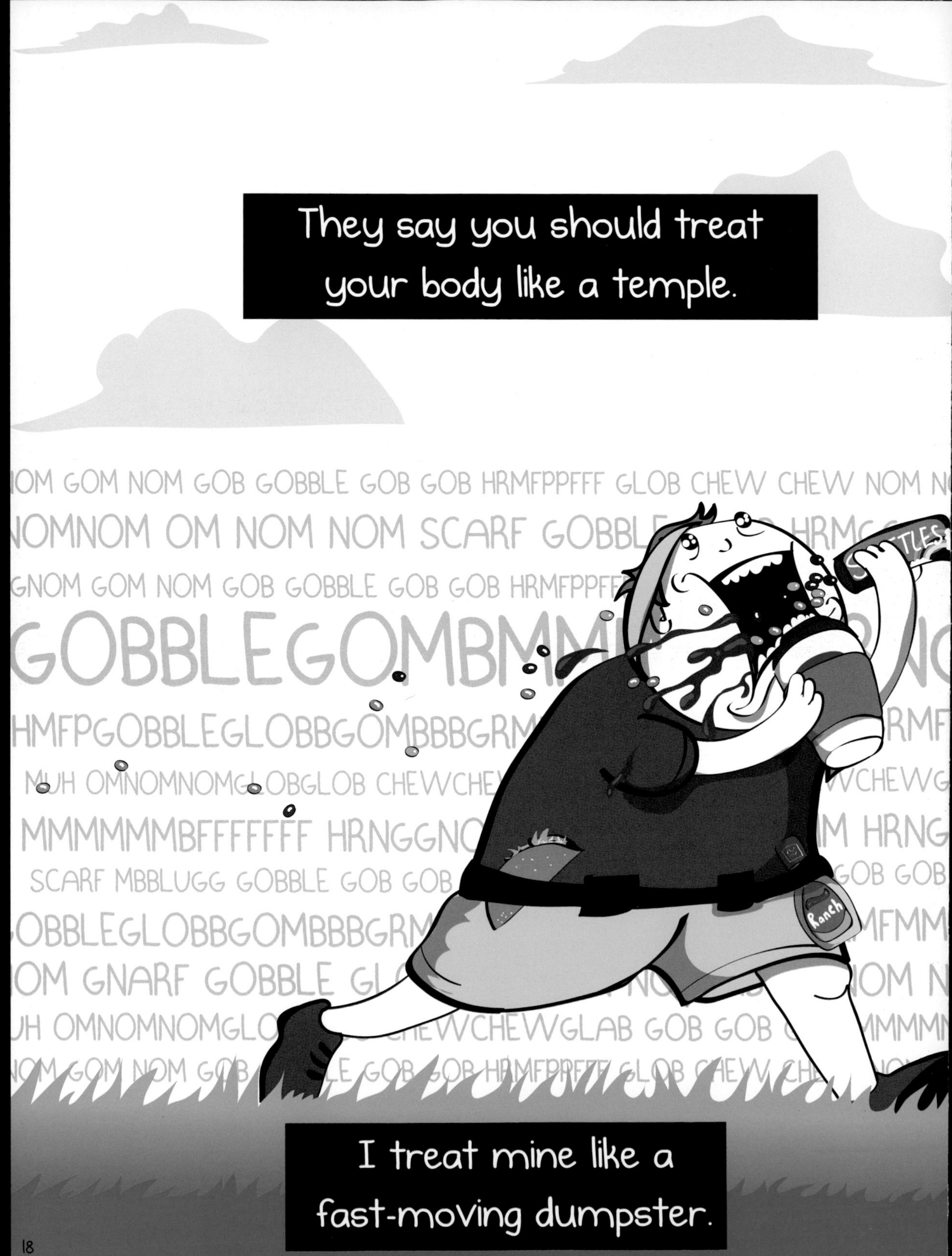
They say you should treat your body like a temple.
Ranch
I treat mine like a fast-moving dumpster.

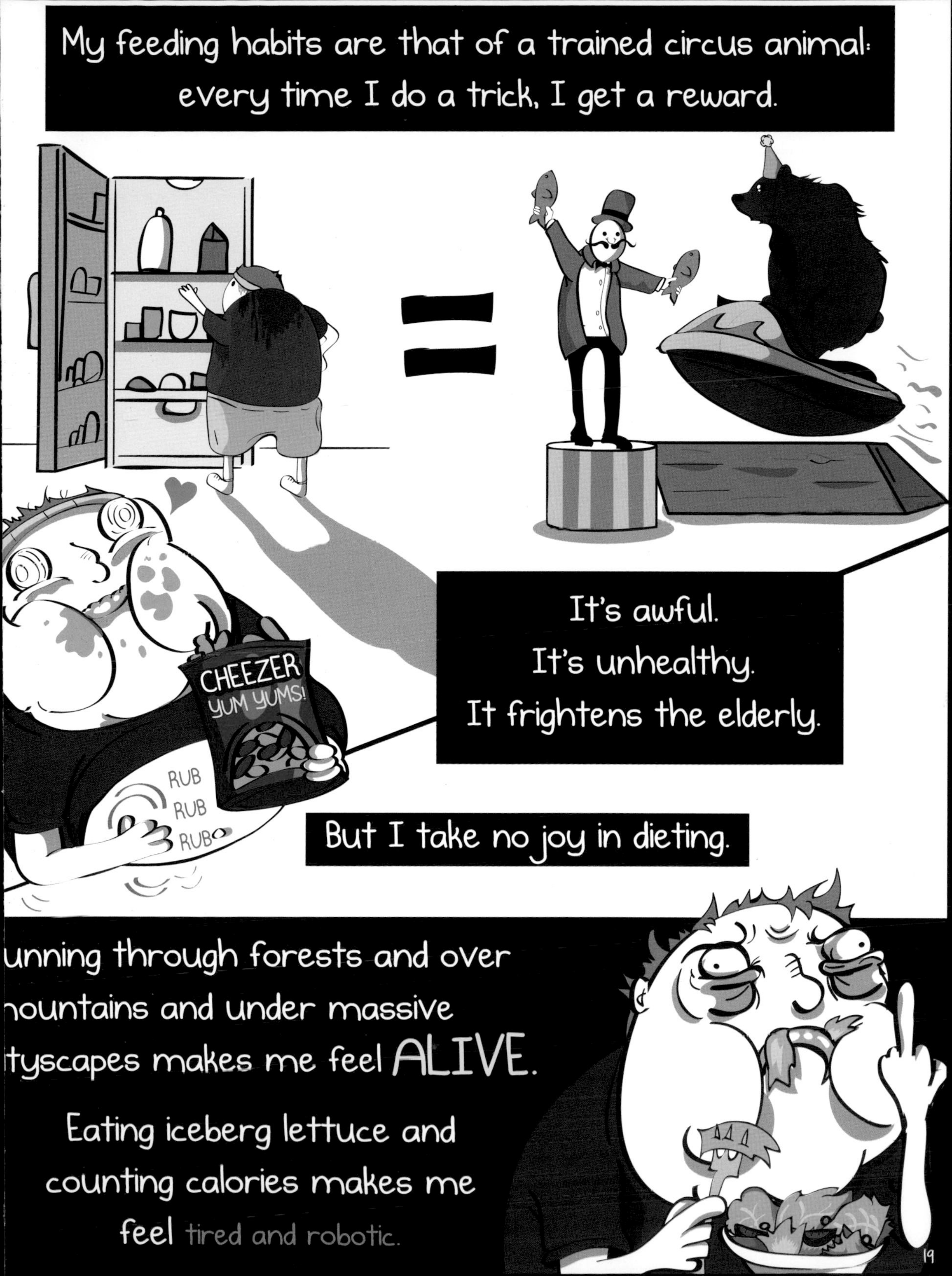
My feeding habits are that of a trained circus animal: every time I do a trick, I get a reward.
CHEEZER YUM YUMS!
RUB RUB RUB
It's awful.
It's unhealthy.
It frightens the elderly.
But I take no joy in dieting.
unning through forests and over
nountains and under massive
ityscapes makes me feel ALIVE.
Eating iceberg lettuce and counting calories makes me feel tired and robotic.

I run long distances for the **worst** possible reason:

I run to eat.

I punish my body outdoors to atone for my atrocities indoors.

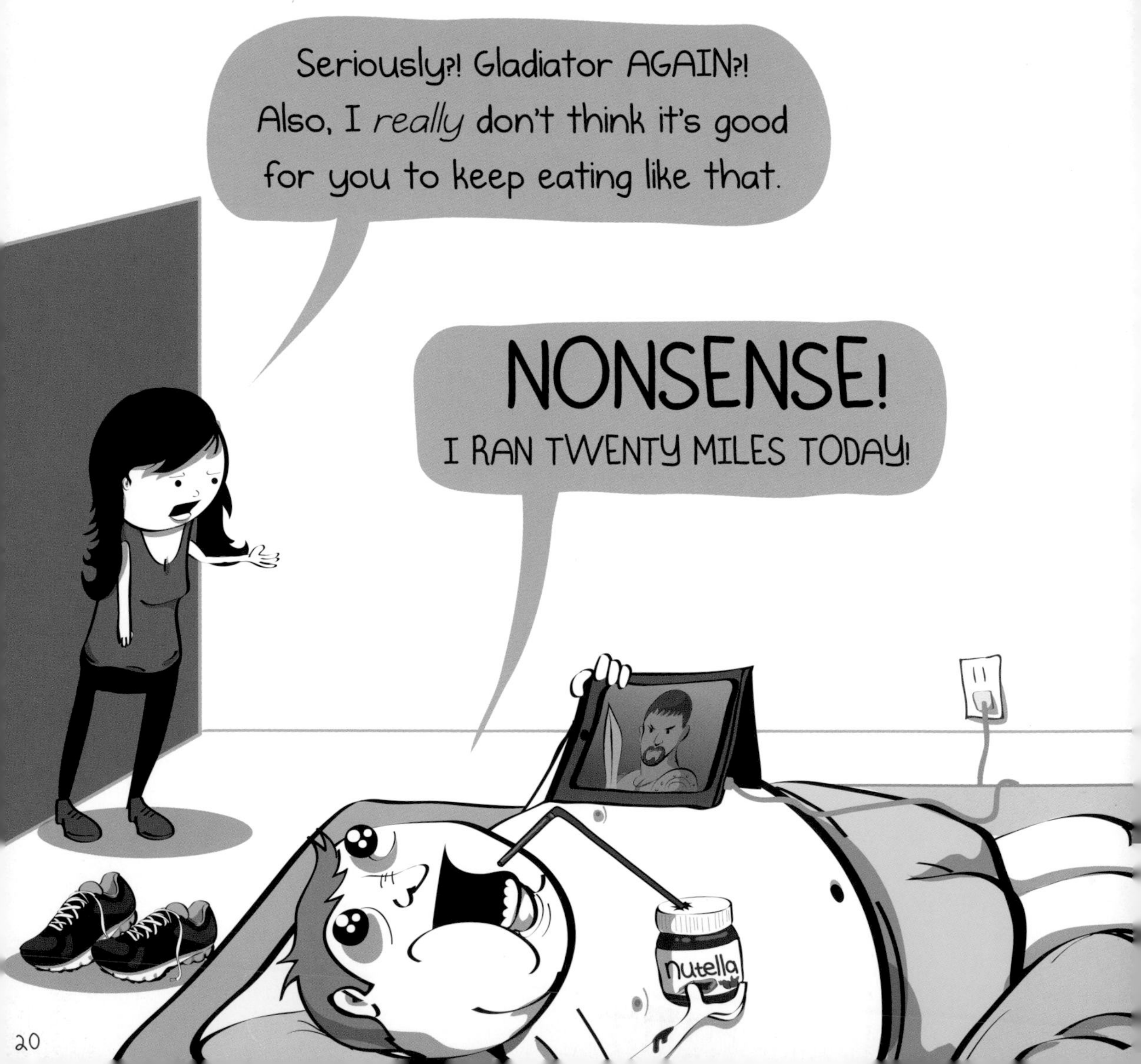

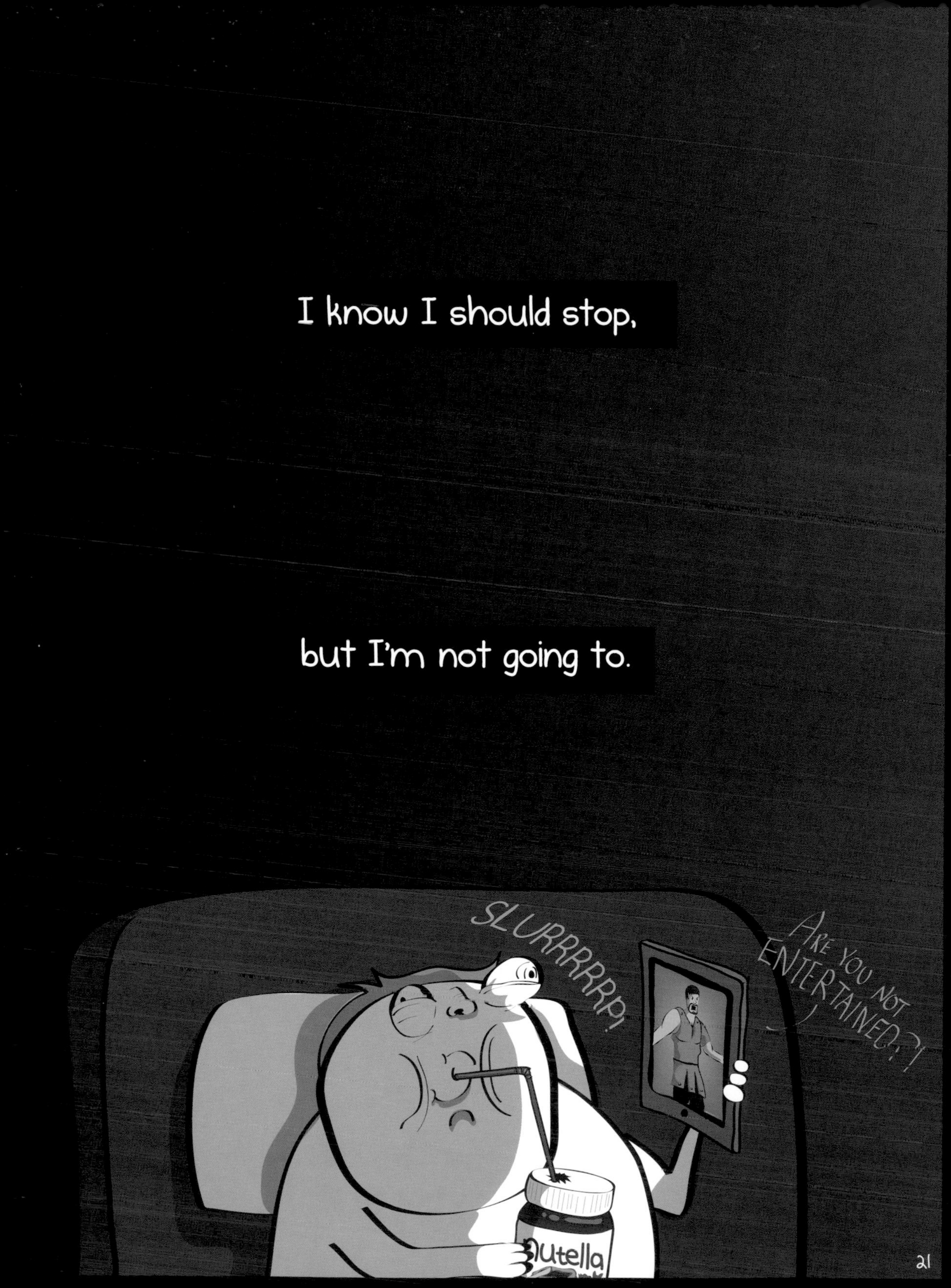
I know I should stop,
but I'm not going to.
SLURRRRRP!
ARE YOU NOT ENTERTAINED?!

Part 3. Selfishness and Krakens

You know how it feels after you pay your bills,
catch up on email,
and clean the entire house?

I love that feeling.
I strive for that idyllic nirvana.

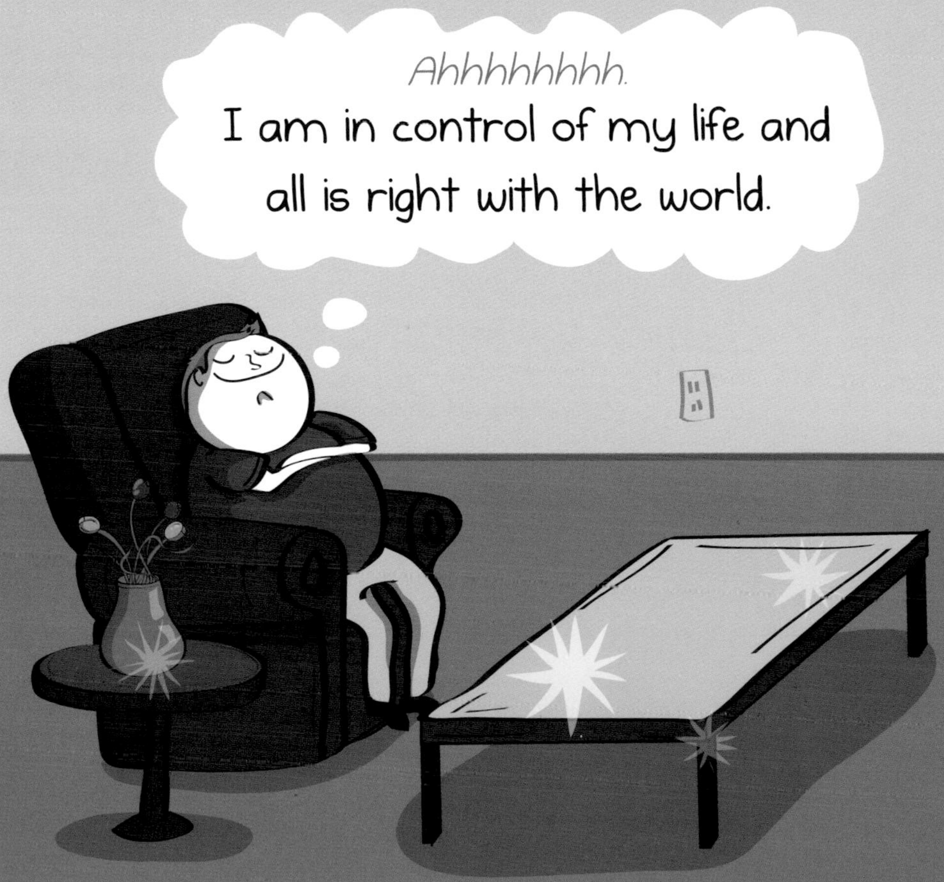
Ahhhhhhhh.
I am in control of my life and
all is right with the world.

The problem is

I don't like paying my bills,
I find replying to emails to be cumbersome,
and I hate cleaning the house.

I like to skip all that crap and go
straight to the nirvana part.

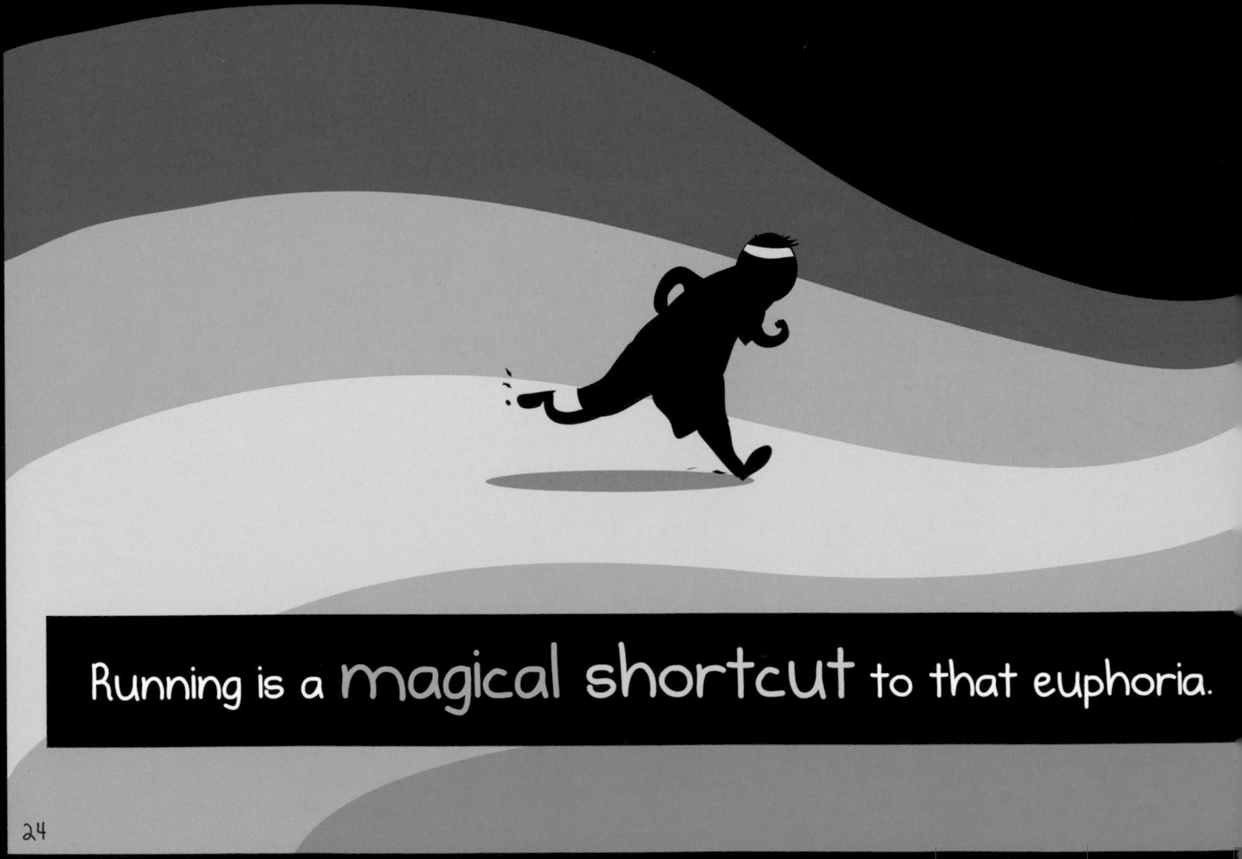
Running is a magical shortcut to that euphoria.

even if it's going straight to hell.

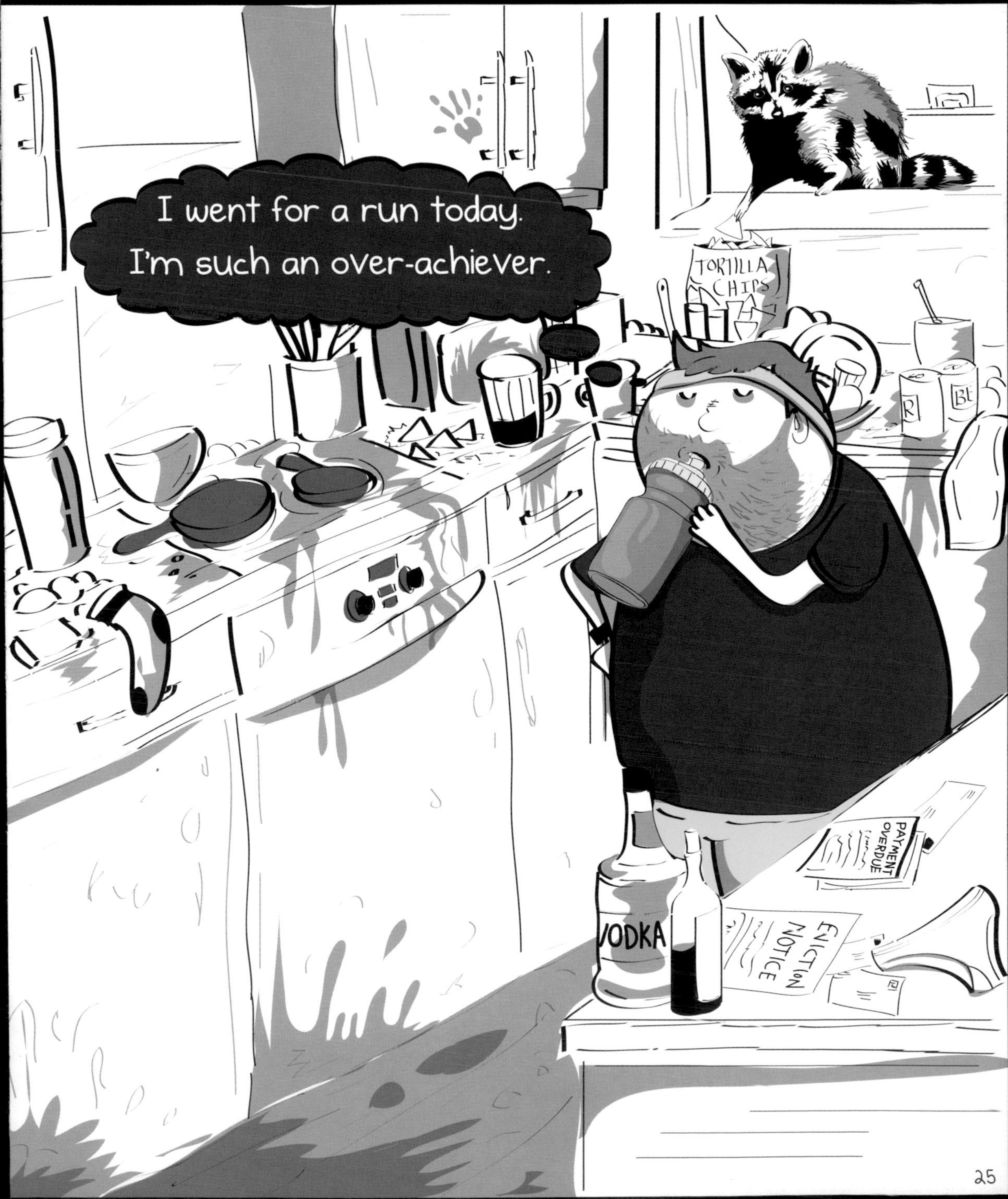
I went for a run today. I'm such an over-achiever.
TORTILLA CHIPS
VODKA
EVICTION NOTICE
PAYMENT OVERDUE

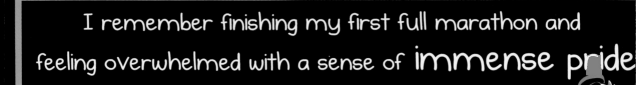

I remember finishing my first full marathon and feeling overwhelmed with a sense of **immense pride**.

I felt like I'd beaten the impossible.

*   I'd ended world hunger.

Found life on Mars.

Defeated the KRAKEN.

FIGHT ME, YOU SILLY BASTARD! I LIVE FOR THE GLORY OF BATTLE!

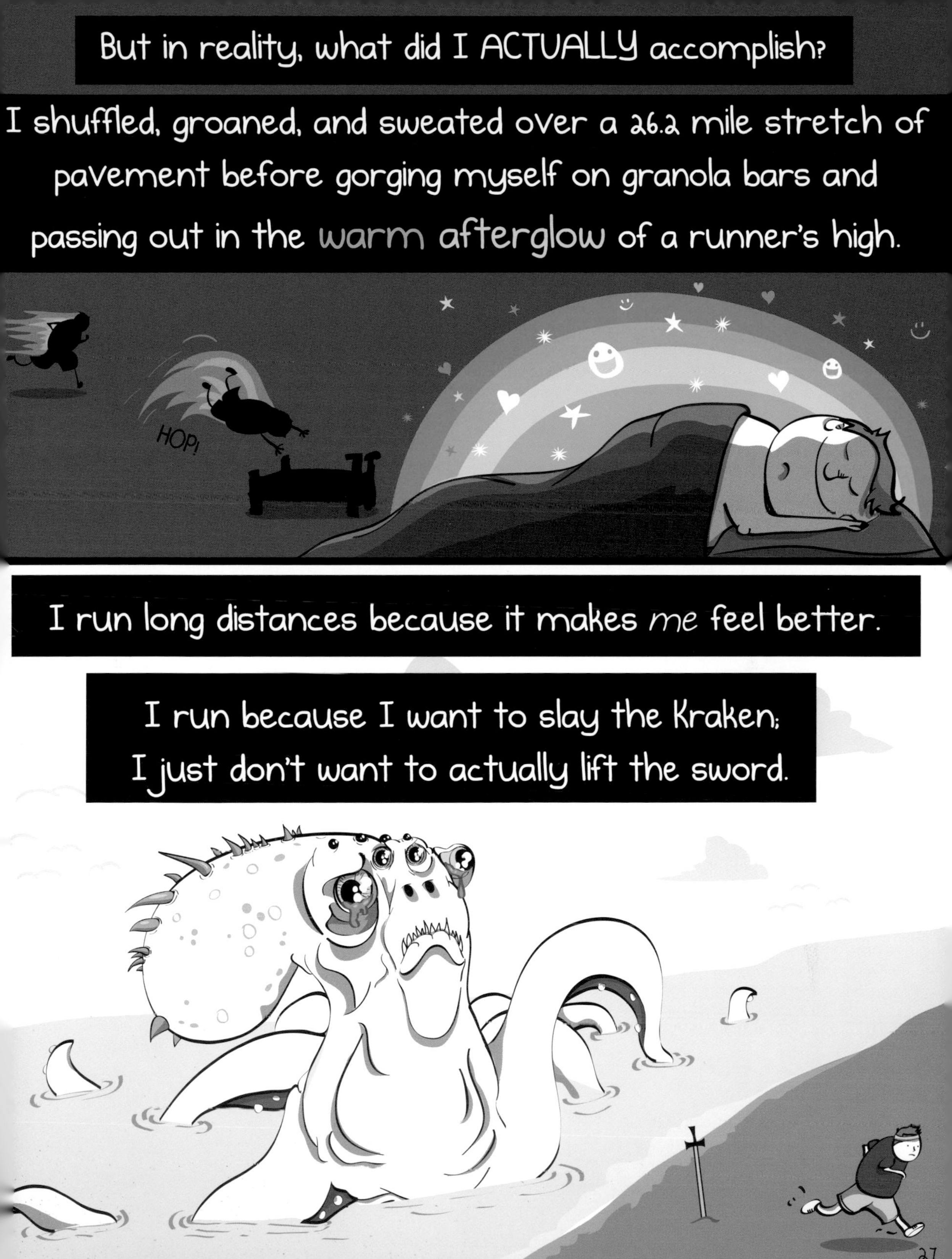
But in reality, what did I ACTUALLY accomplish?
I shuffled, groaned, and sweated over a 26.2 mile stretch of pavement before gorging myself on granola bars and passing out in the warm afterglow of a runner's high.
HOP!
I run long distances because it makes *me* feel better.
I run because I want to slay the Kraken;
I just don't want to actually lift the sword.

Part 4. Vanity

"I read somewhere...
how important it is in life not necessarily
to **be** strong, but to *feel* strong...
to measure yourself at least once."

- Christopher McCandless
from Jon Krakauer's *Into the Wild*

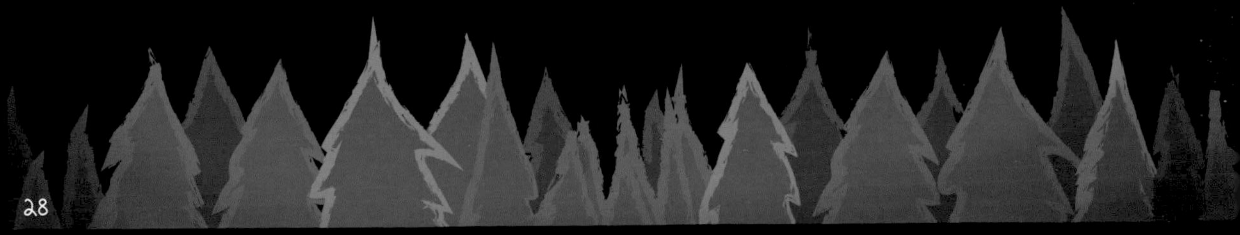

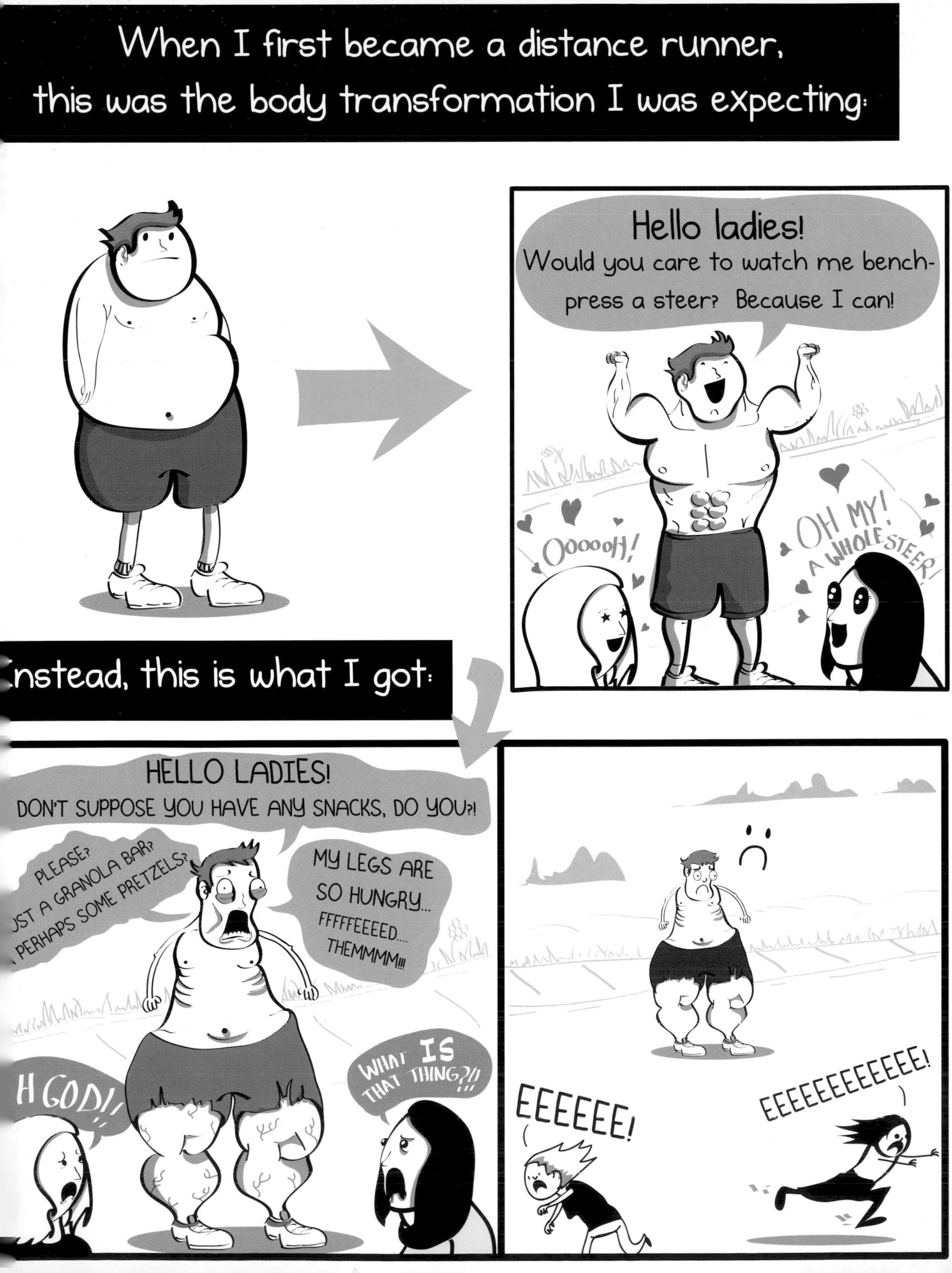
When I first became a distance runner, this was the body transformation I was expecting:
Hello ladies!
Would you care to watch me bench-press a steer? Because I can!
OOOooH!
OH MY! A WHOLE STEER!
Instead, this is what I got:
HELLO LADIES!
DON'T SUPPOSE YOU HAVE ANY SNACKS, DO YOU?!
PLEASE? JUST A GRANOLA BAR? PERHAPS SOME PRETZELS?
MY LEGS ARE SO HUNGRY... FFFFFEEEED.... THEMMMM!!!
H GOD!!
WHAT IS THAT THING?!!
EEEEEE!
EEEEEEEEEEEE!

Running is not about vanity.

If I wanted to look good I'd get a gym membership and stand in front of a mirror doing bicep curls.

I'd go tanning and drink protein shakes and participate in all the other synchronized stupidity that has come to embody **bad gym culture.**

Take, for example, stomach crunches:

Crunches are an exercise where you lie on your back and angrily try to head-butt your crotch.

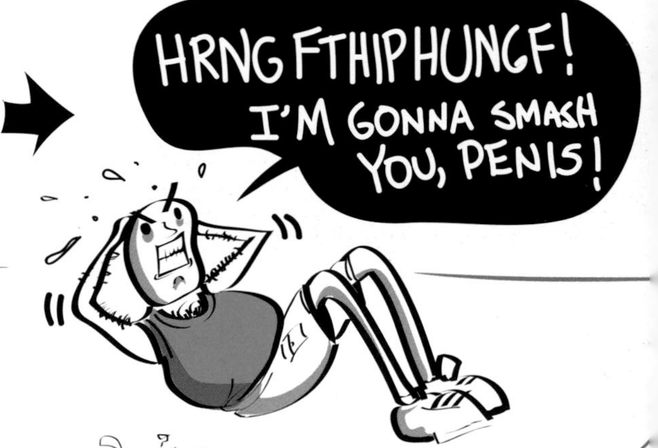
HRNG FTHIPHUNGF!
I'M GONNA SMASH YOU, PENIS!

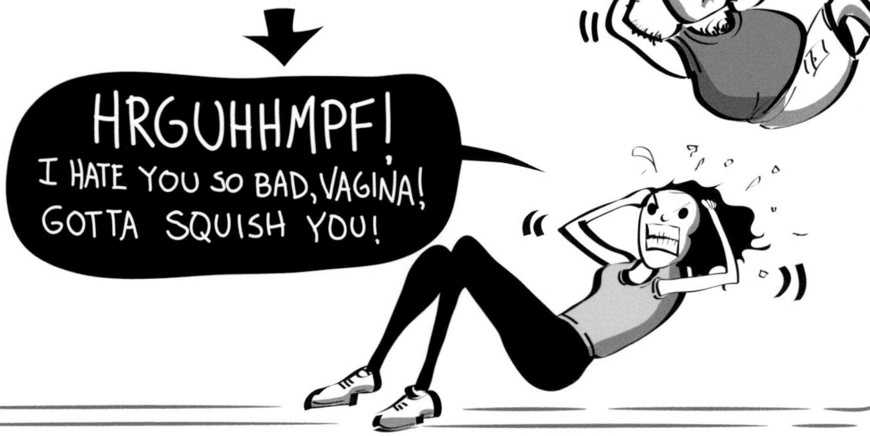
HRGUHHMPF!
I HATE YOU SO BAD, VAGINA!
GOTTA SQUISH YOU!

They're uncomfortable, bad for your back, they do nothing for your core, and they're purely **vanity-driven**: people only do crunches because they want six pack abs.

(Never mind the fact that even if you do ten million crunches a day, you'll never see your abs unless you diet like crazy and drop your body fat percentage.)

But people do them anyway. They line up on the gym floor and pound away at their privates like frantic little hamsters.

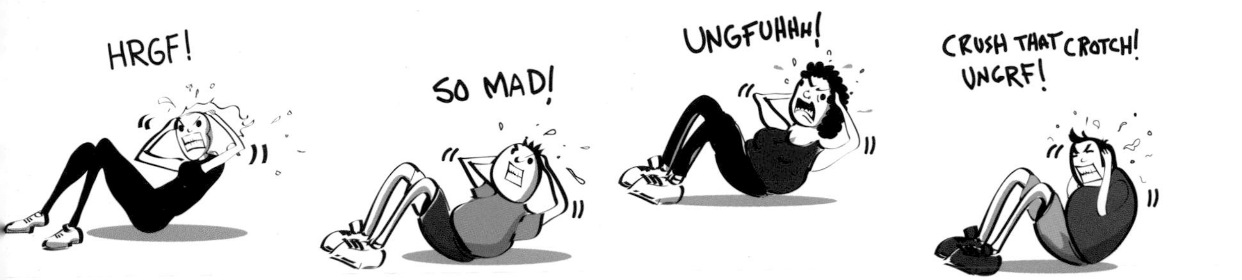
HRGF!
SO MAD!
UNGFUHHH!
CRUSH THAT CROTCH!
UNGRF!

These are the same people who read beauty magazines while jogging on ellipticals and drinking Diet Coke. They wax their chests and wear stupidly tight muscle shirts and painfully obsess over all the superficial details of the fragile little carbon-based-meat-suitcases known as their BODIES.

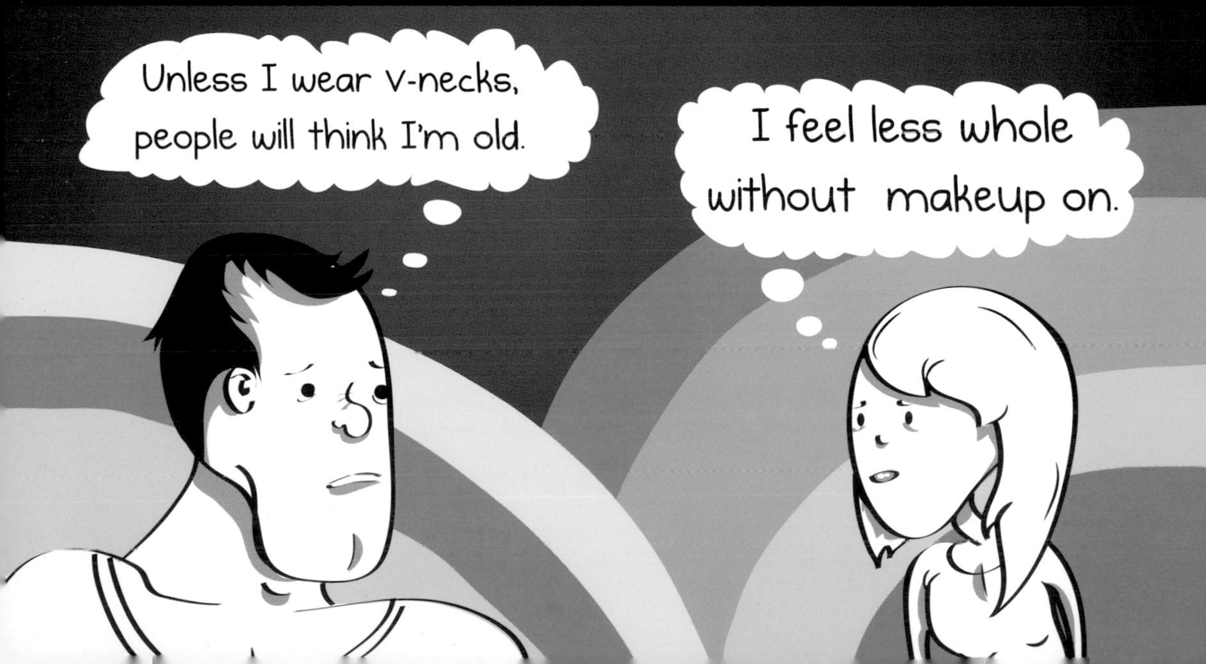
Unless I wear V-necks, people will think I'm old.
I feel less whole without makeup on.

These types of people also tend to spend a lot of time lying down in these things:

If you are considering entering a tanning bed, I have some advice for you:

Do not fall into this thing.

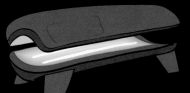

Fall into something *real* instead.

Fall into a good book.

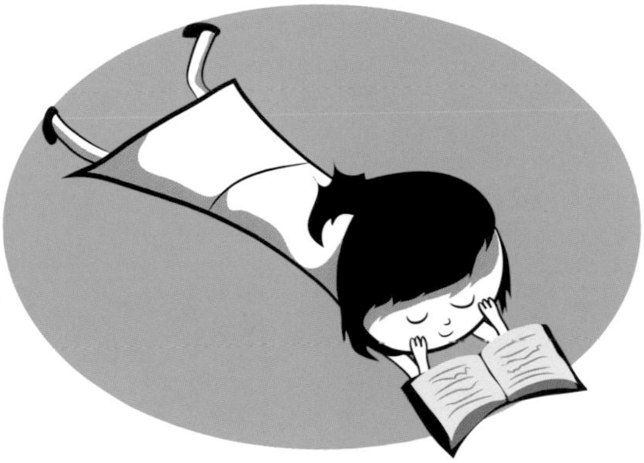

Fall in love.

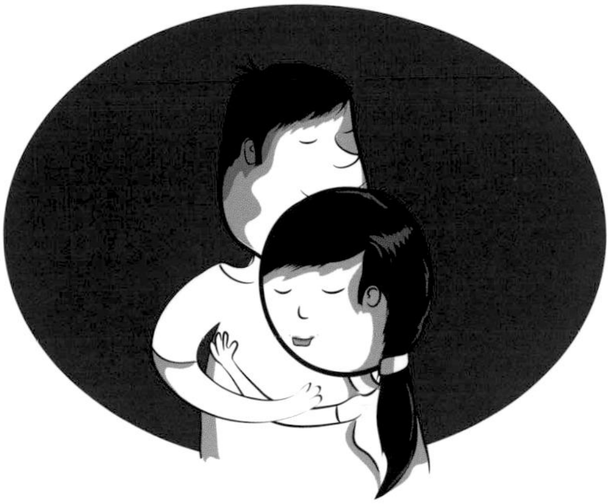

Fall out of love.

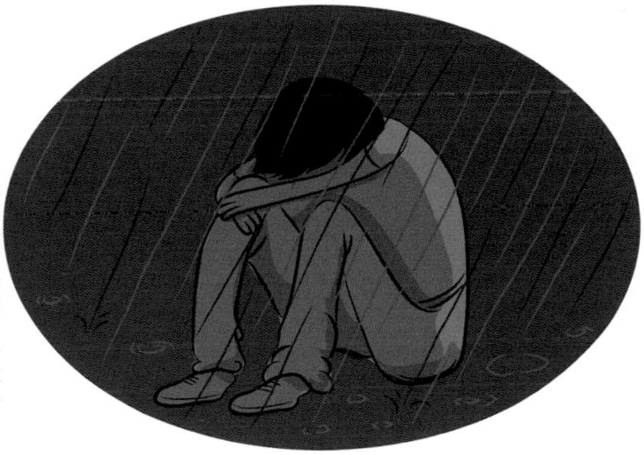

Fall into a hole.

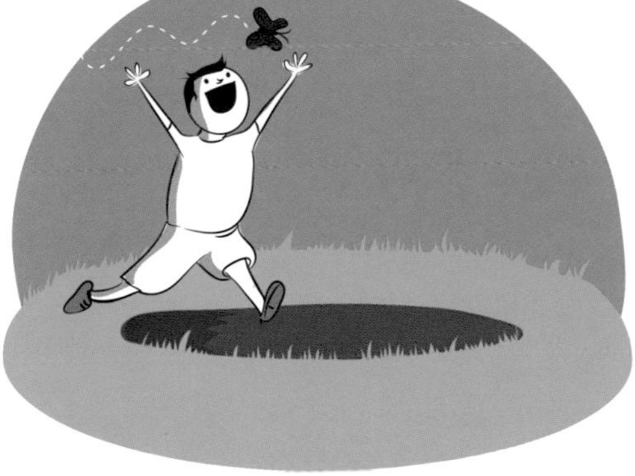

Fall into something.

Fall into ANYTHING of consequence.

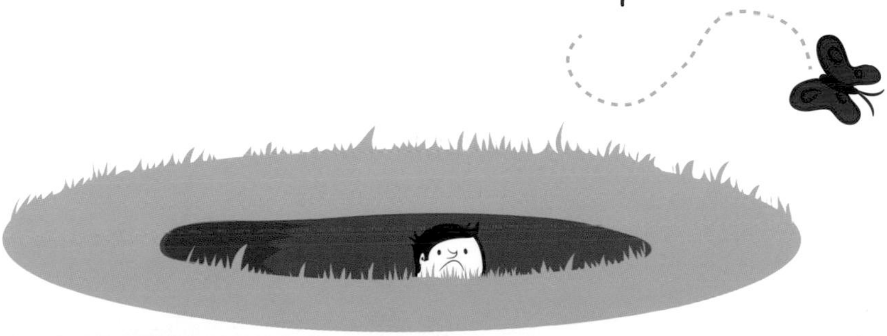

Just don't fall into a tanning bed.

These machines are for vapid, narcissistic idiots who have barren vacuums where their thoughts, fears, and passions should be.

Spending time in a tanning bed will only earn you the appearance and intellect of an inbred baked potato.

GOTTA GET FIT AND TAN SO I CAN HOLLA UP IN THA CLUB!

Don't be a baked potato.
Be a person.

Narcissistic baked potatoes are the antithesis of why I run.

Running is not about building strength and wearing it like a fashion statement.

It's about *finding* strength and *measuring* yourself every single day.

I run long distances to *feel* good, not to *look* good.

I run long distances because I am not, nor shall I ever be, a baked potato.

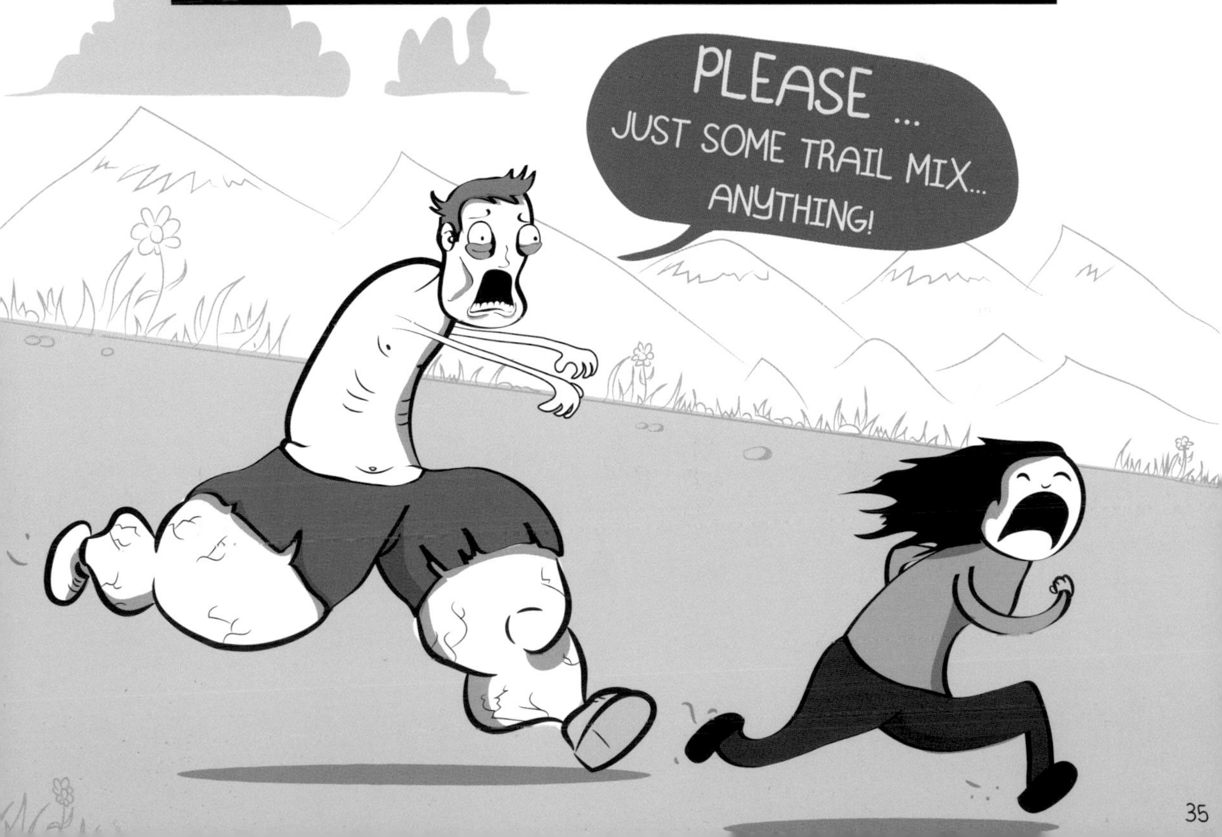
PLEASE ... JUST SOME TRAIL MIX... ANYTHING!

Part 5. The Agony

One of the most
terrible and **wonderful**
runs of my life happened several years ago in Japan.

It was hot: 104° Fahrenheit (40°C) with full humidity.

I was running up a mountain that was nestled against a large city, and, because of the intense heat, this mountain was completely devoid of hikers

—so I was alone.

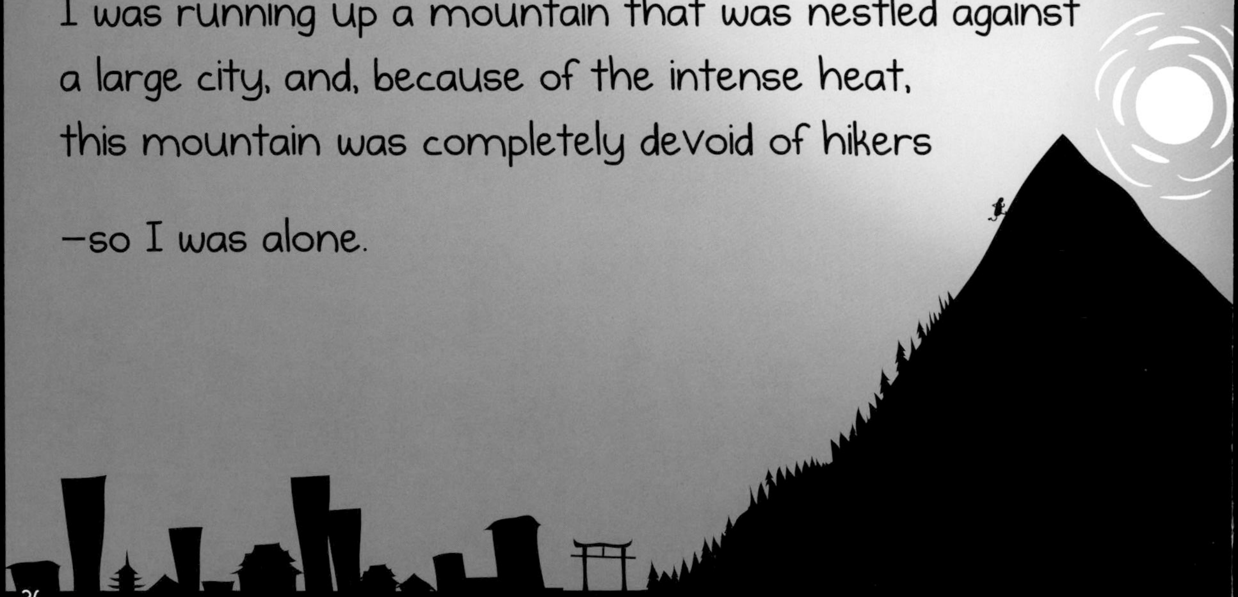

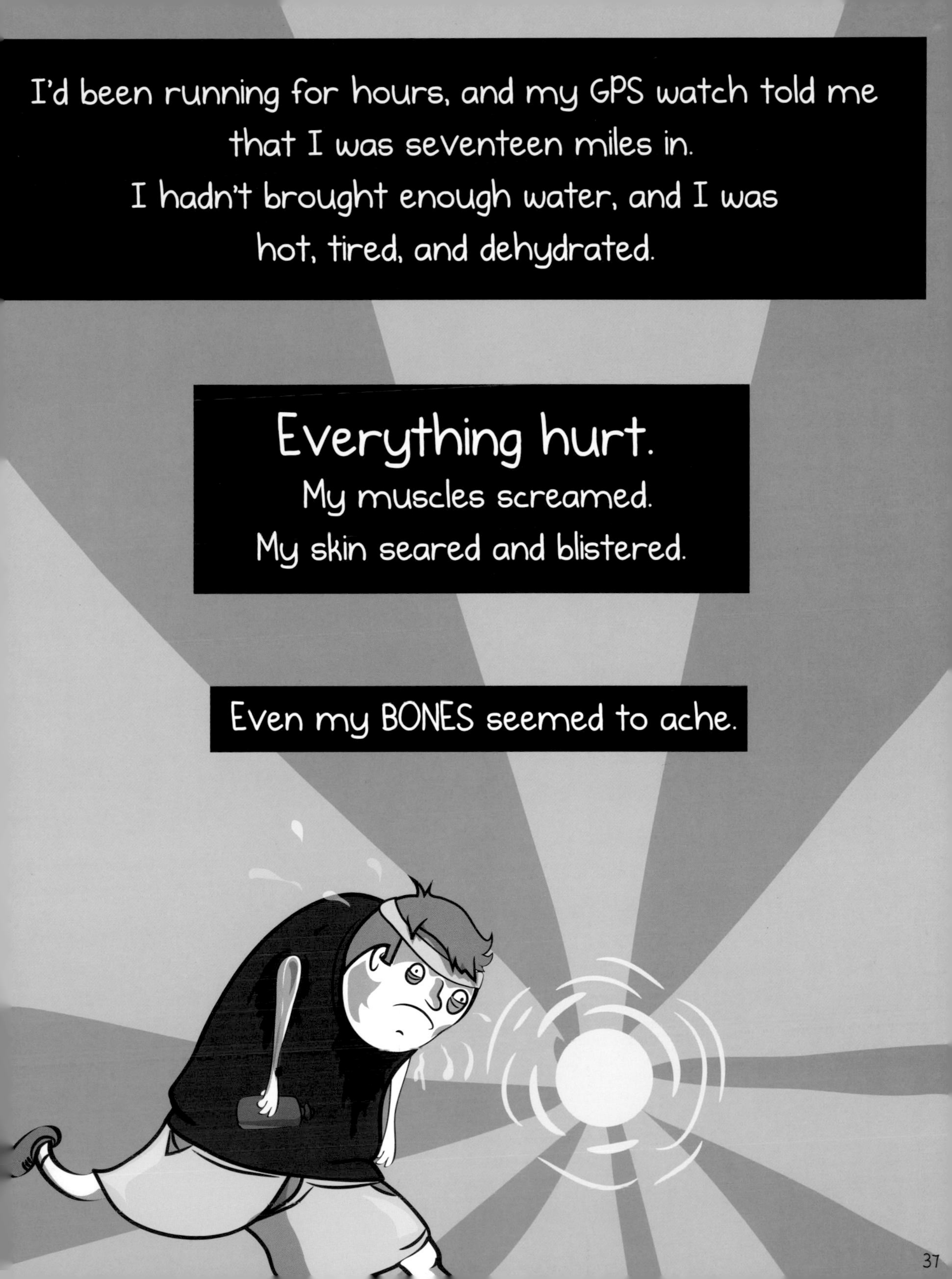
I'd been running for hours, and my GPS watch told me that I was seventeen miles in.
I hadn't brought enough water, and I was hot, tired, and dehydrated.
Everything hurt.
My muscles screamed.
My skin seared and blistered.
Even my BONES seemed to ache.

At the base of this mountain was a massive bamboo forest which, although beautiful, was home to an army of **Japanese giant hornets.**

Japanese people call these hornets *Oo-Suzumebachi* (オオスズメバチ) which translates to "Giant Sparrow Bees," due to the fact that they're huge—almost the size of your thumb.

These hornets have stingers which are 1/4" long (6.25 mm) and can deliver venom that melts human flesh. The sting, which is considered to be one of the most painful on earth, is so bad it'll put you in the hospital.

On average, Japanese giant hornets kill 40 people a year, making them the most lethal animal in the country.

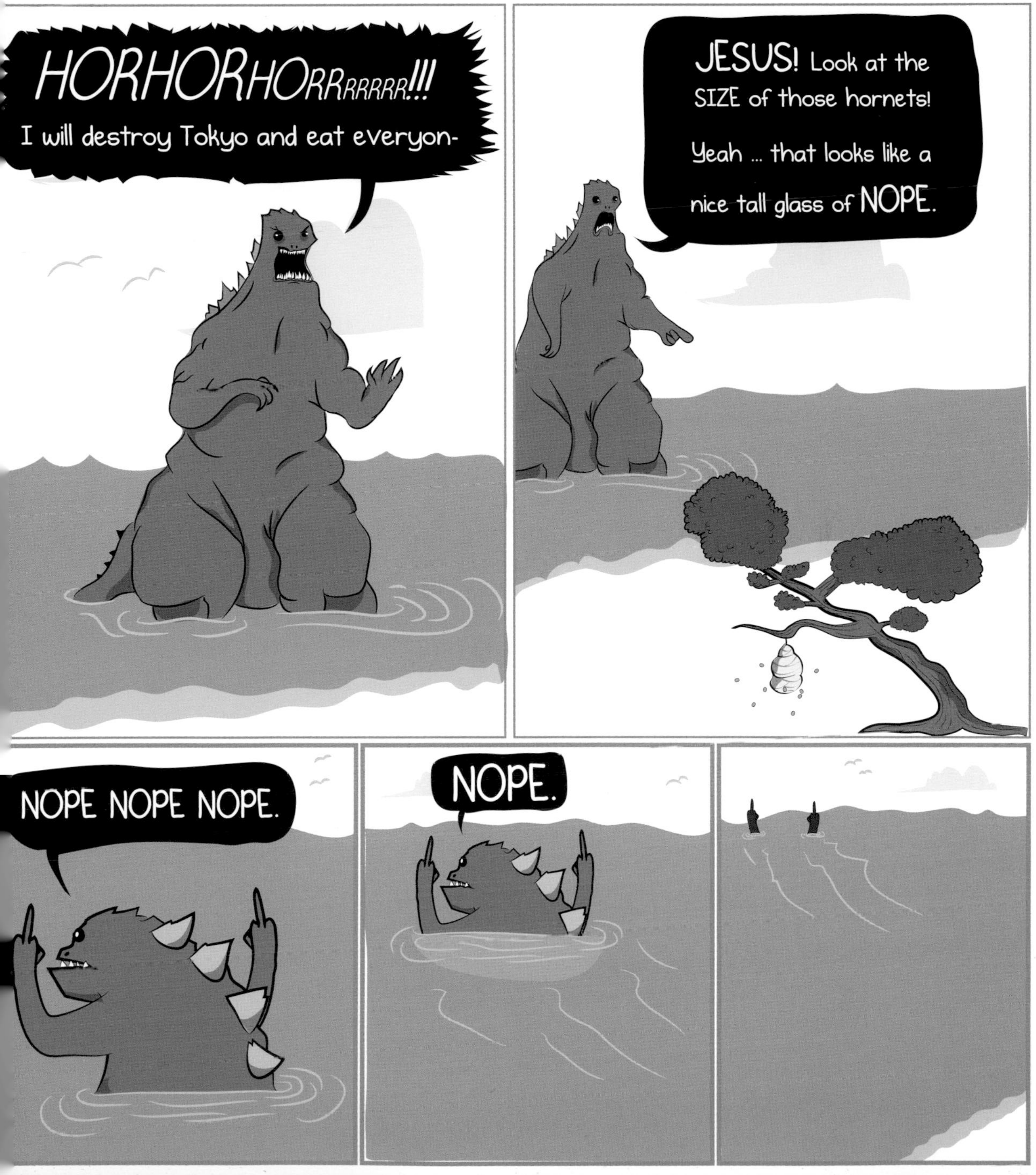
HORHORHORRRRRRR!!!
I will destroy Tokyo and eat everyon-
JESUS! Look at the SIZE of those hornets!
Yeah ... that looks like a nice tall glass of NOPE.
NOPE NOPE NOPE.
NOPE.

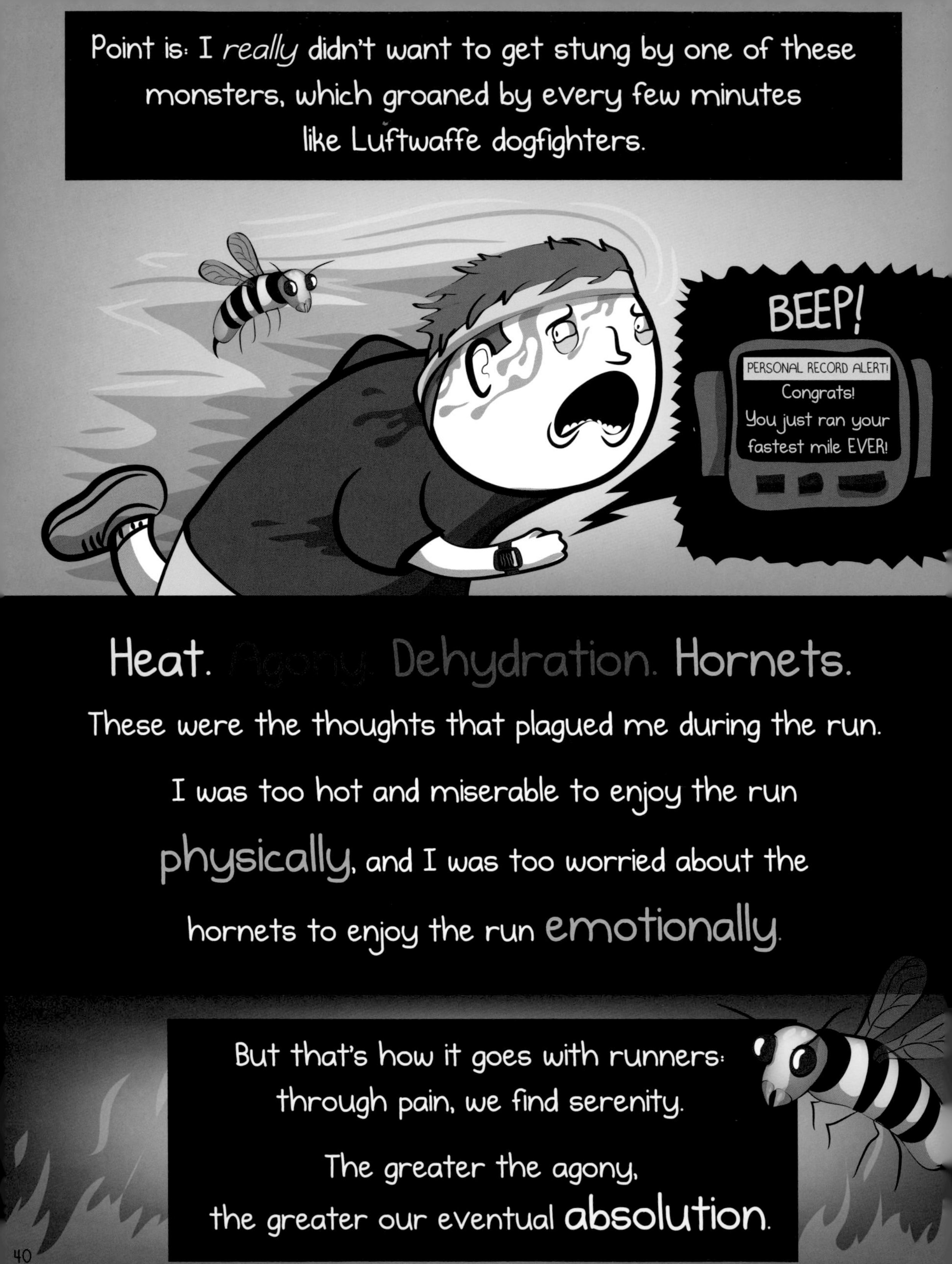
Point is: I *really* didn't want to get stung by one of these monsters, which groaned by every few minutes like Luftwaffe dogfighters.
BEEP!
PERSONAL RECORD ALERT!
Congrats!
You just ran your fastest mile EVER!
Heat. Agony. Dehydration. Hornets.
These were the thoughts that plagued me during the run.
I was too hot and miserable to enjoy the run physically, and I was too worried about the hornets to enjoy the run emotionally.
But that's how it goes with runners: through pain, we find serenity.
The greater the agony, the greater our eventual absolution.

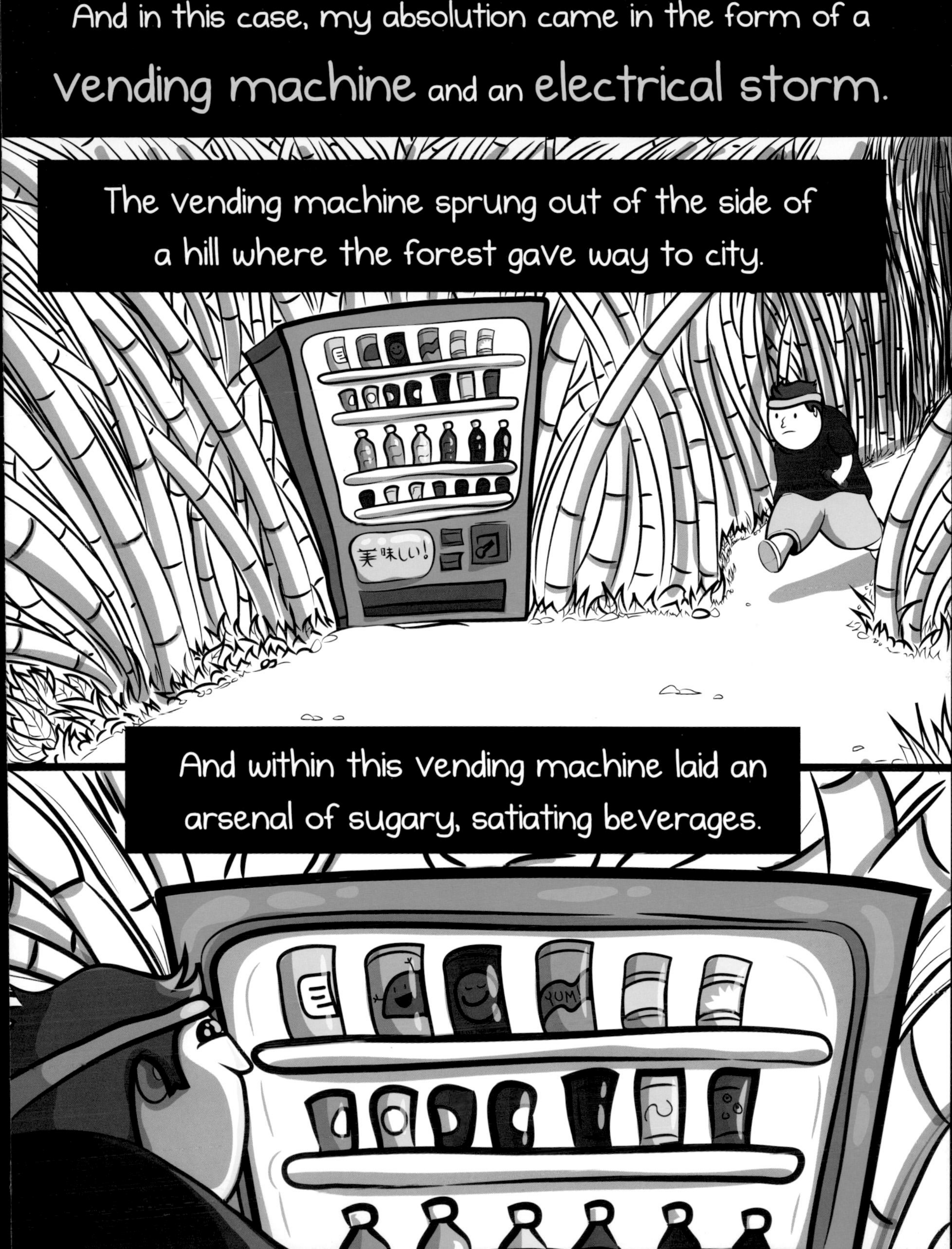
And in this case, my absolution came in the form of a vending machine and an electrical storm.
The vending machine sprung out of the side of a hill where the forest gave way to city.
美味しい!
And within this vending machine laid an arsenal of sugary, satiating beverages.
YUM!

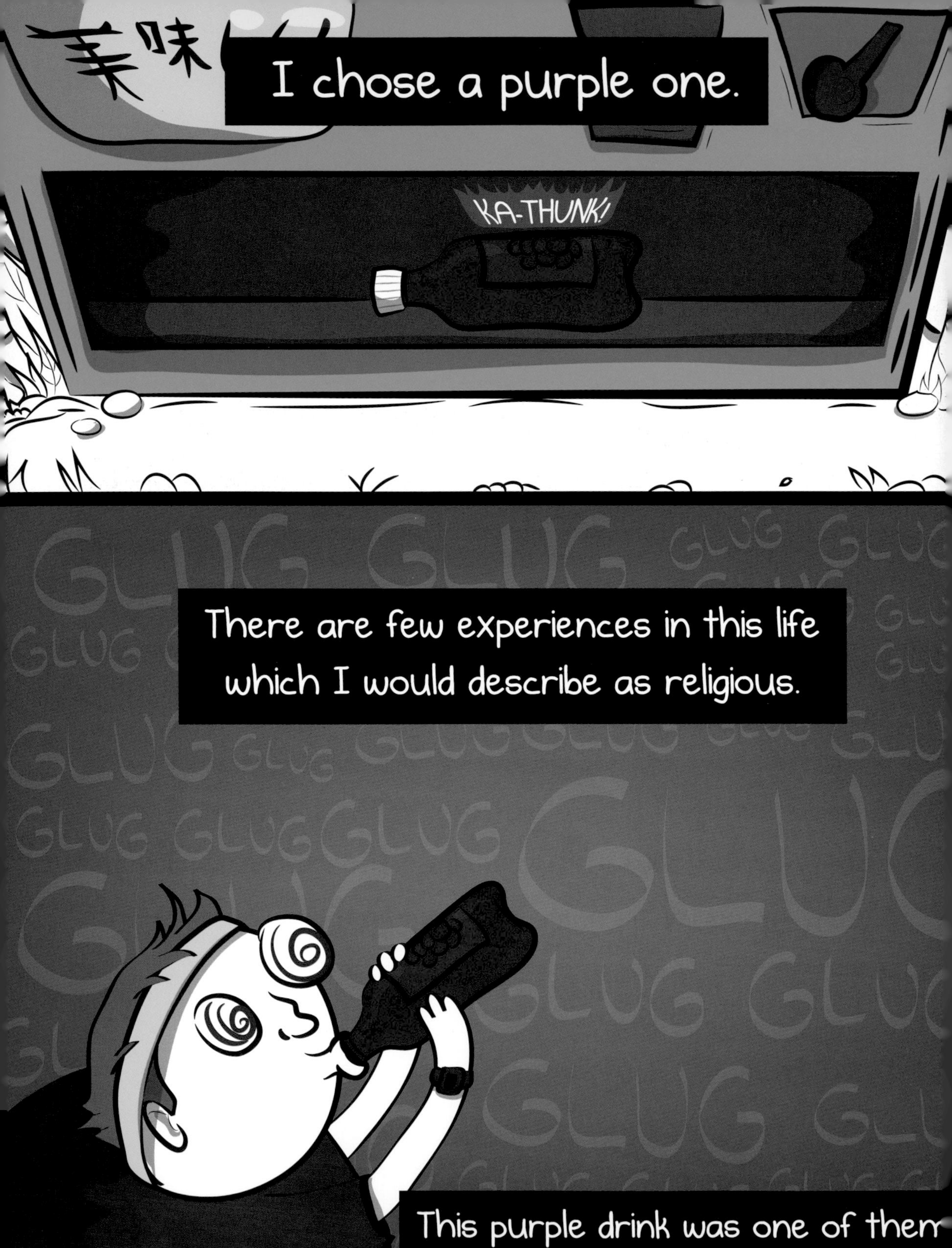
美味
I chose a purple one.
KA-THUNK!
GLUG GLUG GLUG GLUG
There are few experiences in this life which I would describe as religious.
This purple drink was one of them

It tasted like the souls of
ten thousand unborn panda bears.

It tasted like someone stole the balls off a
pegasus and blended them into a smoothie.

It tasted like sugar, water, and absolution.

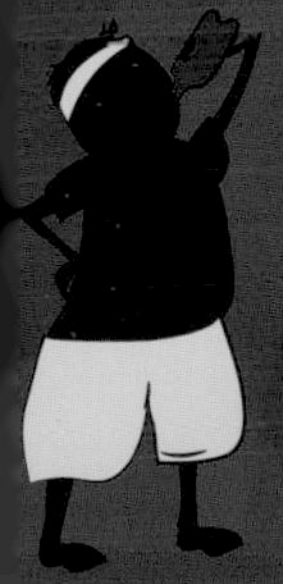

It tasted good.

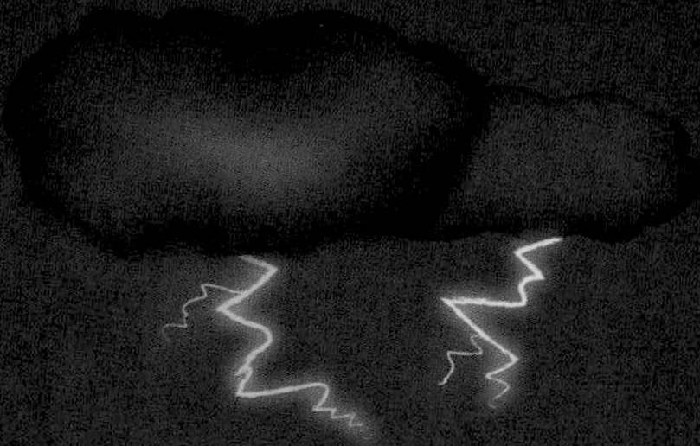

Part 6. The Void

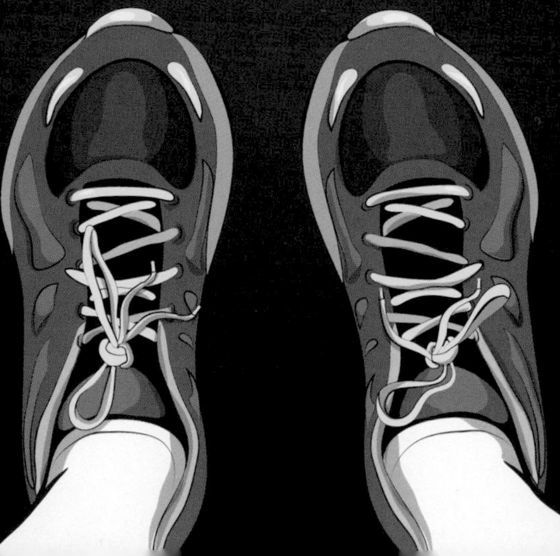

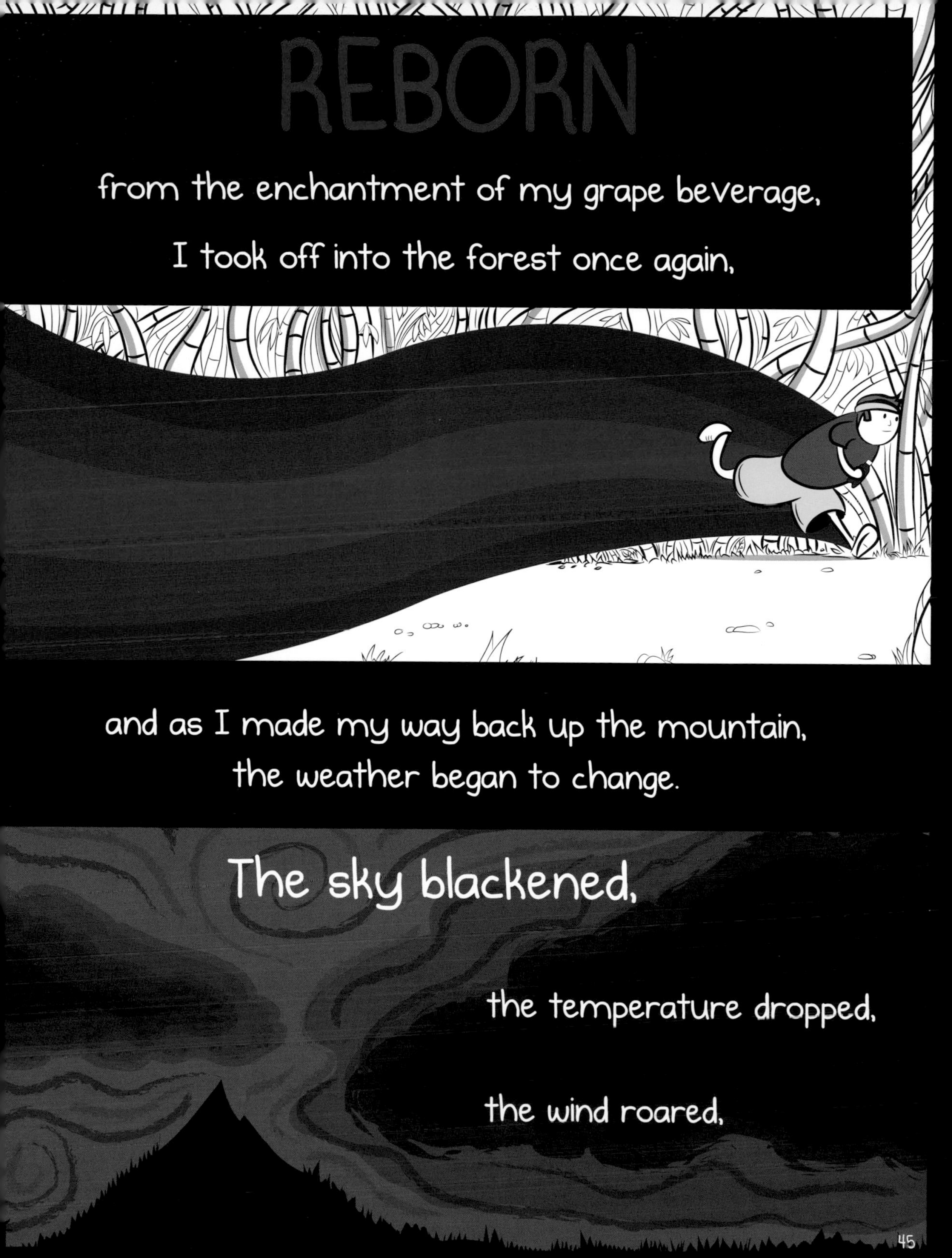
REBORN
from the enchantment of my grape beverage,
I took off into the forest once again,
and as I made my way back up the mountain,
the weather began to change.
The sky blackened,
the temperature dropped,
the wind roared,

and the bamboo trees began to CRASH into each other,

groaning and snapping and wailing in **agony**.

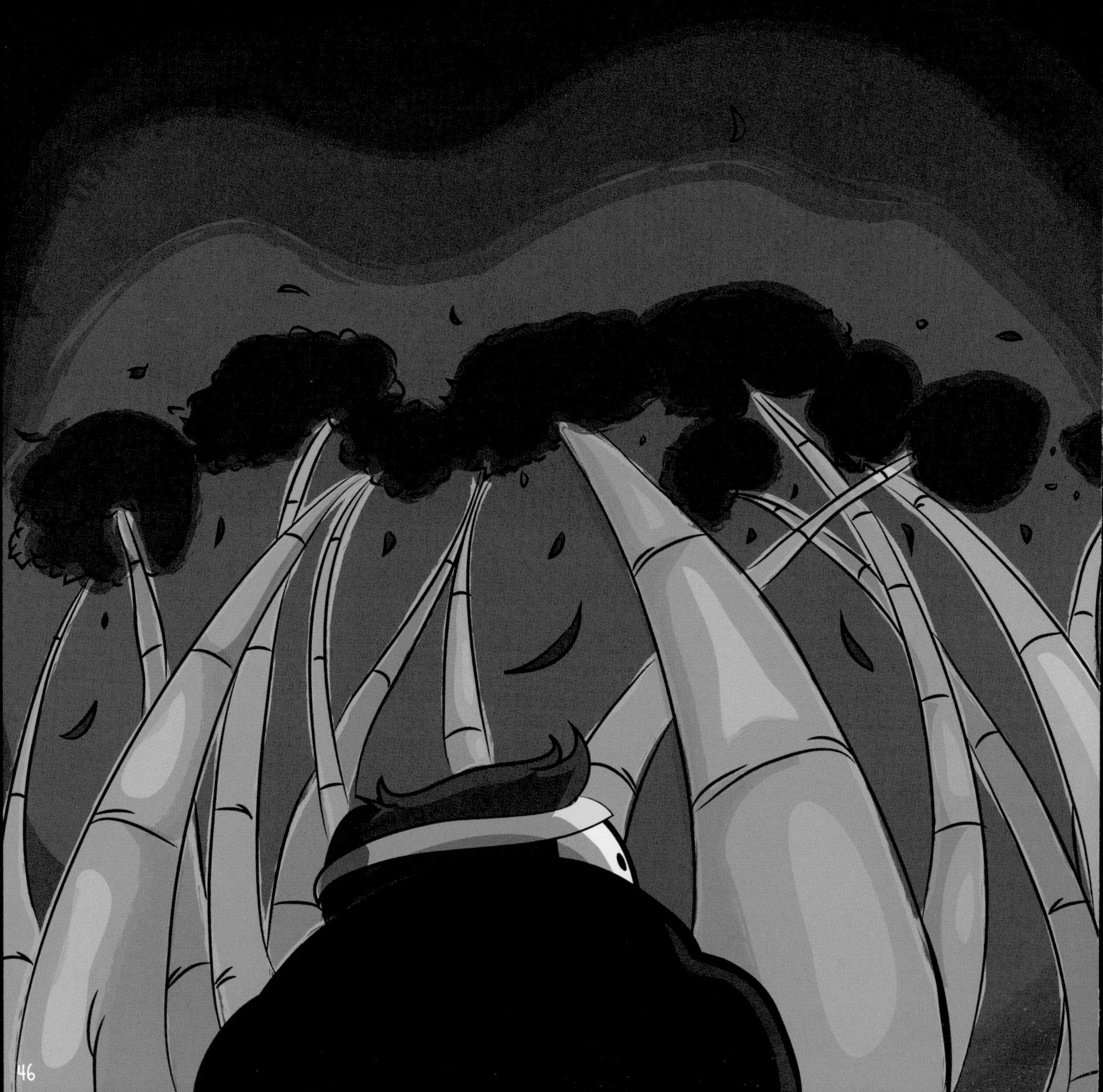

ghtning **exploded** over the treetops,

nd rain began to fall.

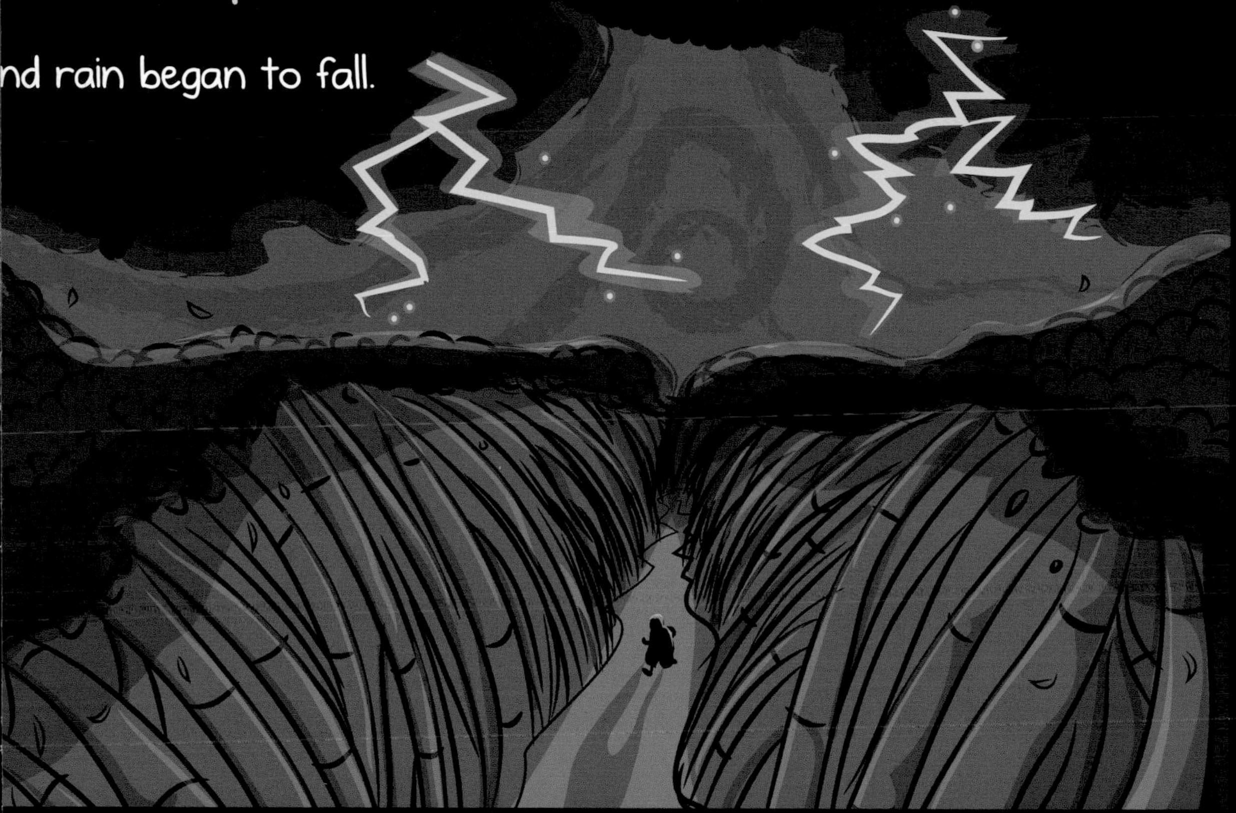

The hornets fled the forest,

and that kingdom of heat and worry and torment
which had belonged to those nightmare insects
became a kingdom of **bliss**, which belonged to **me**.

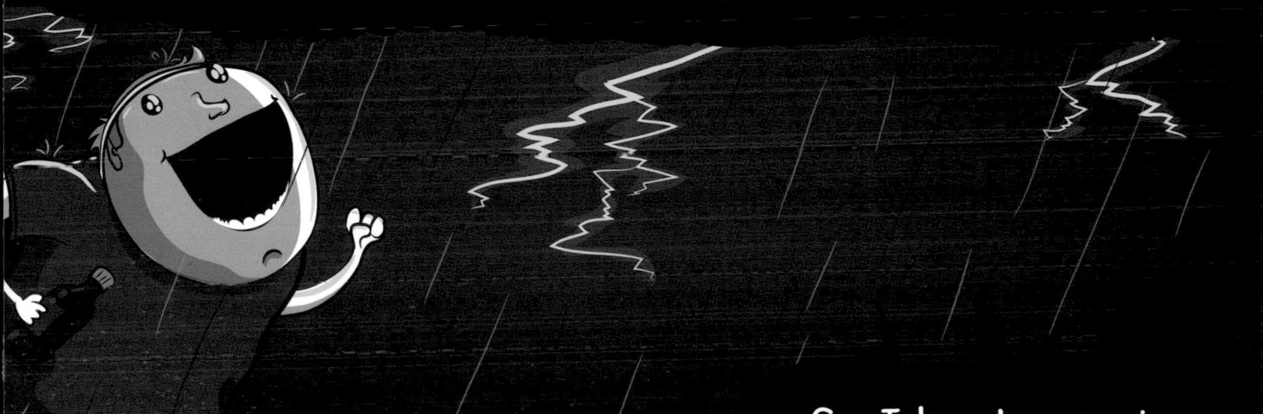

So I kept running.

It was on this day,
during this terrible and wonderful run,
that a thought occurred to me,
a thought which has never left me:

I've always considered *the* question to be

"Why am I alive? Why am I here

What's the point of *me*?"

And to that I say:

WHO CARES!

FORGET THE *WHY*.

YOU ARE IN A RAGING FOREST
FULL OF **BEAUTY** AND **AGONY** AND
MAGICAL GRAPEY BEVERAGES AND

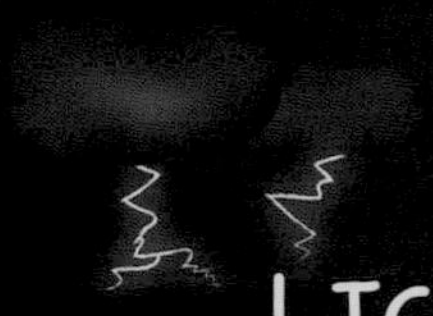

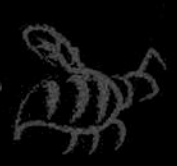

LIGHTNING STORMS AND DEMON BEES.

THIS IS BETTER THAN THE *WHY*.

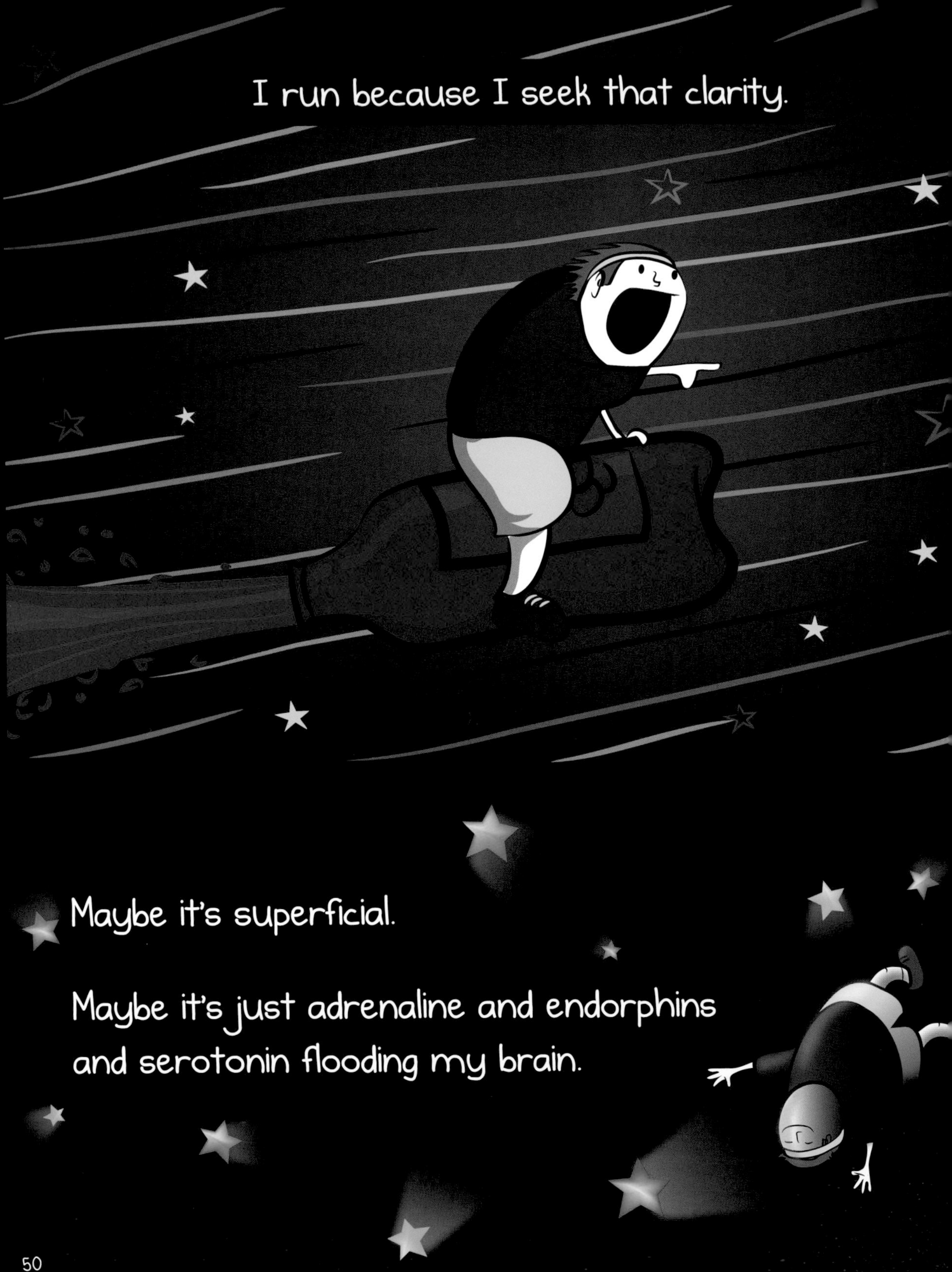
I run because I seek that clarity.
Maybe it's superficial.
Maybe it's just adrenaline and endorphins and serotonin flooding my brain.

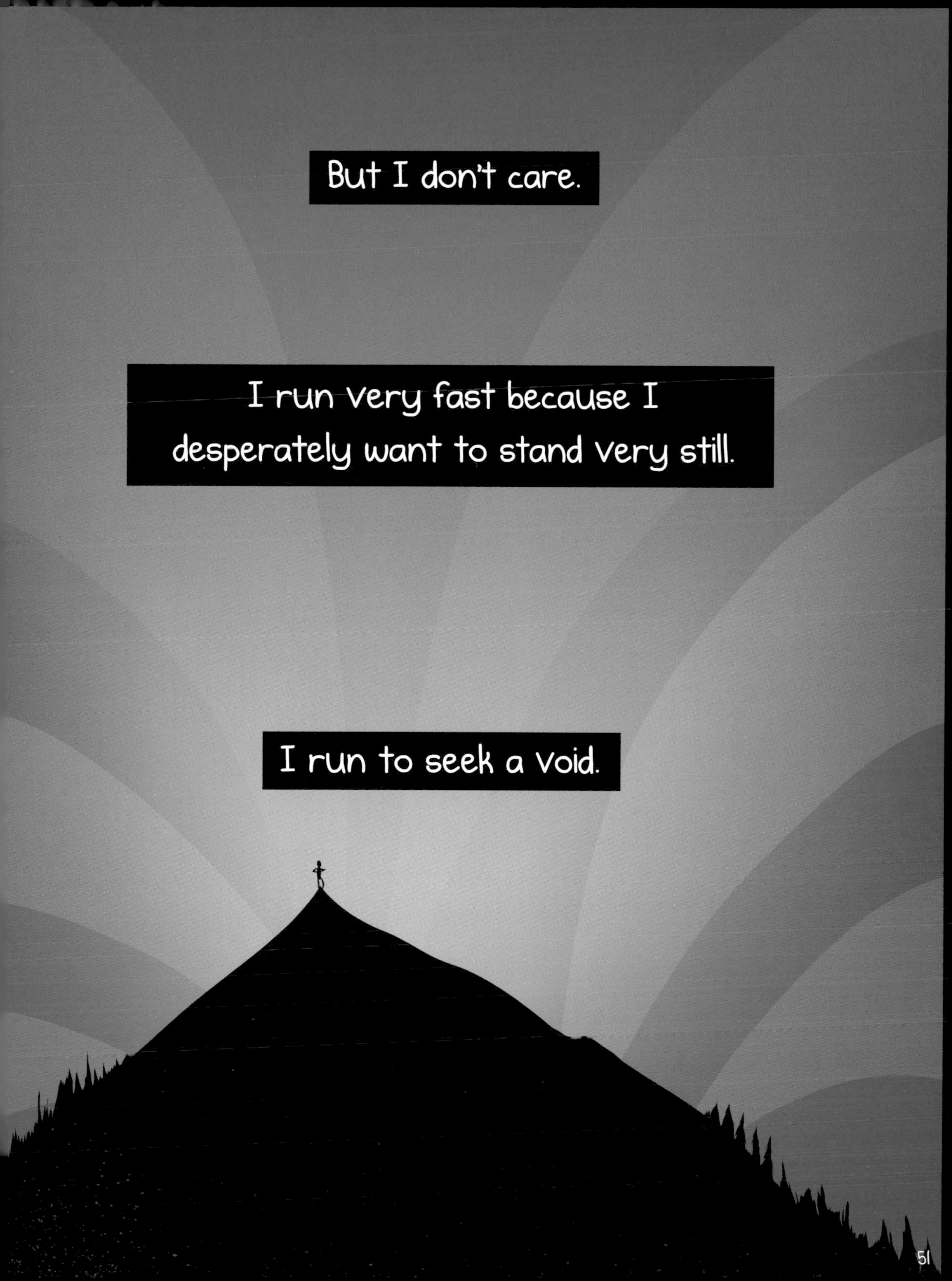
But I don't care.
I run very fast because I desperately want to stand very still.
I run to seek a void.

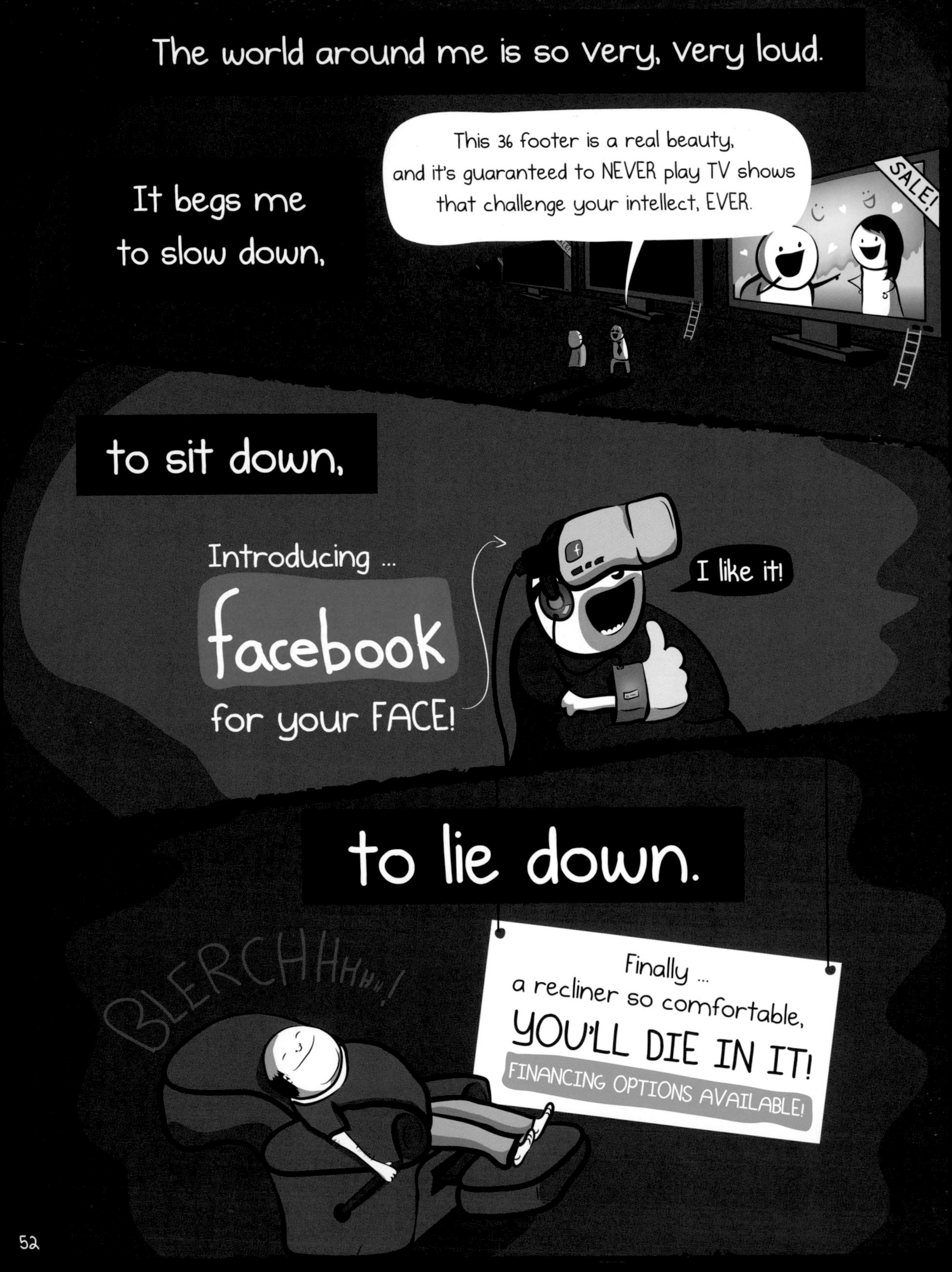

The world around me is so very, very loud.
It begs me to slow down,
This 36 footer is a real beauty, and it's guaranteed to NEVER play TV shows that challenge your intellect, EVER.
SALE!
to sit down,
Introducing ...
facebook
for your FACE!
I like it!
to lie down.
BLERCHHhhh!
Finally ... a recliner so comfortable, YOU'LL DIE IN IT!
FINANCING OPTIONS AVAILABLE!

And the buzzing roar of the world is nothing compared to the noise inside my head. I'm an introspective person, and sometimes I think too much, about my job and about my life.

I feed an army of pointless, bantering demons.

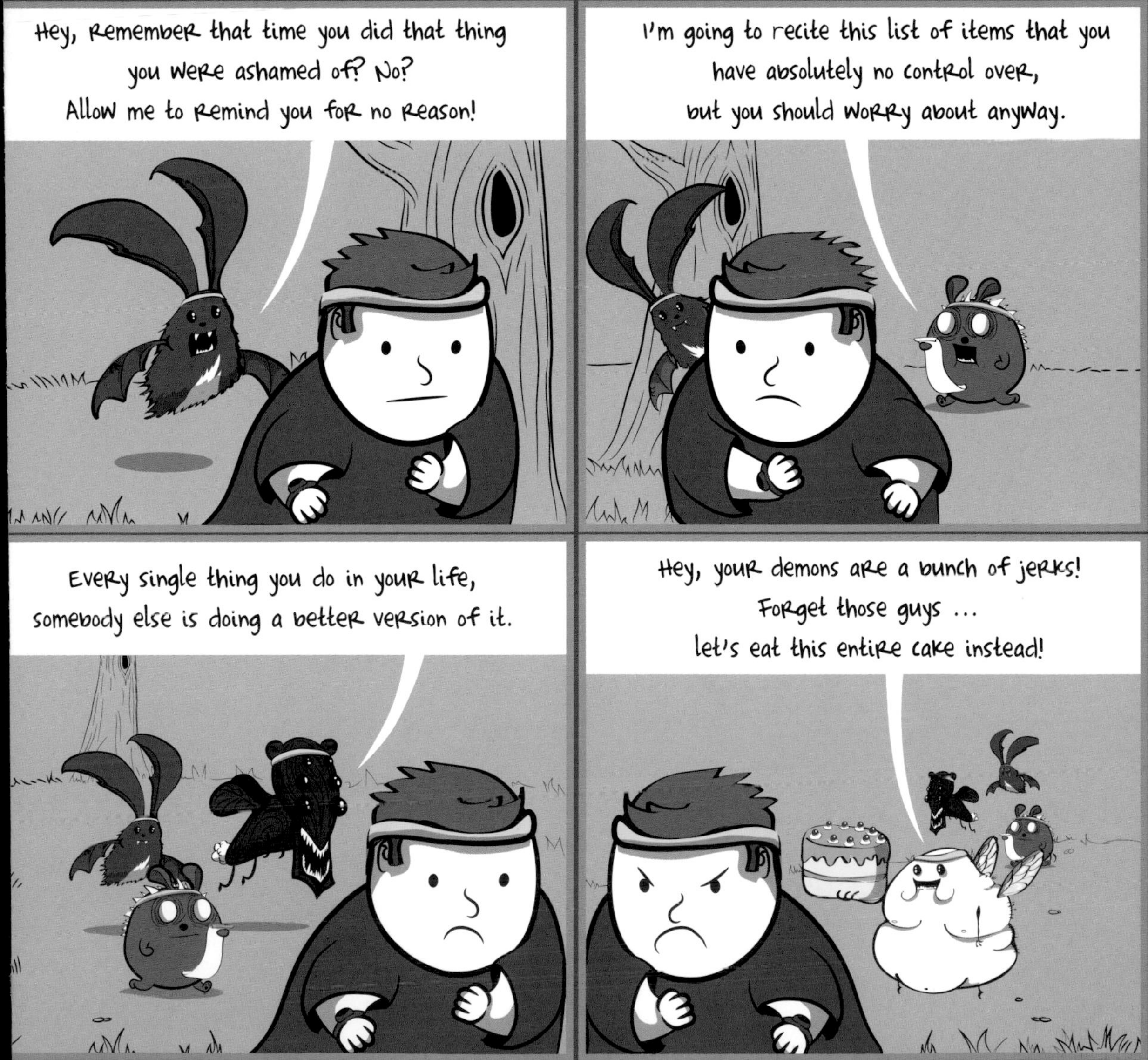

Hey, remember that time you did that thing you were ashamed of? No? Allow me to remind you for no reason!
I'm going to recite this list of items that you have absolutely no control over, but you should worry about anyway.
Every single thing you do in your life, somebody else is doing a better version of it.
Hey, your demons are a bunch of jerks! Forget those guys ... let's eat this entire cake instead!

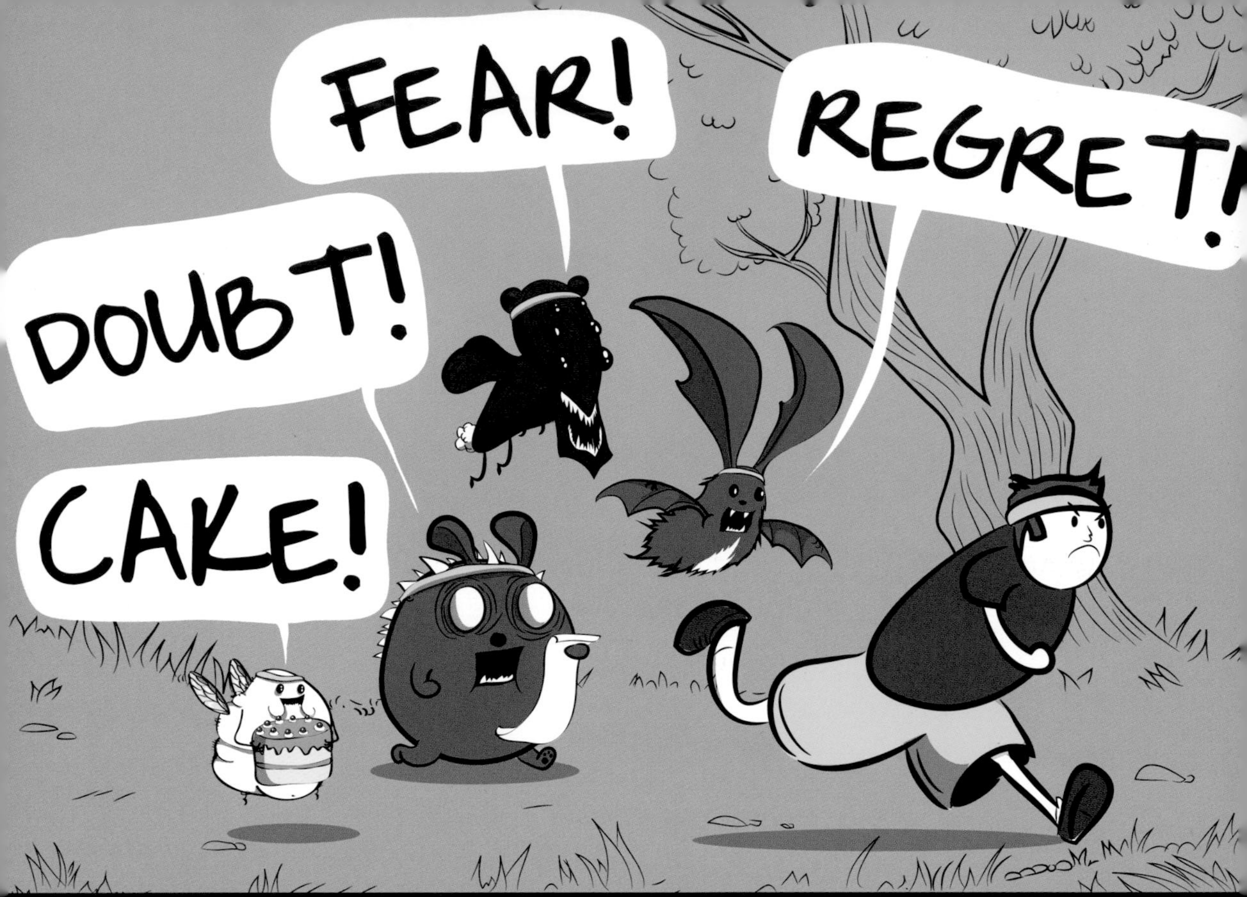
FEAR!
REGRET!
DOUBT!
CAKE!

But when I run, the world grows quiet.

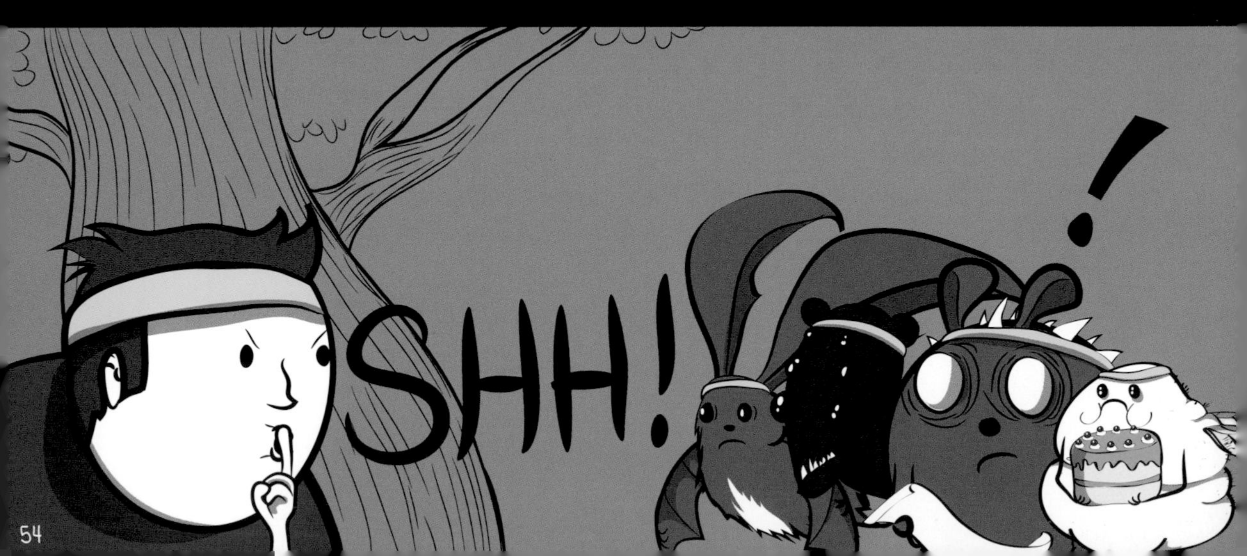
SHH!
!

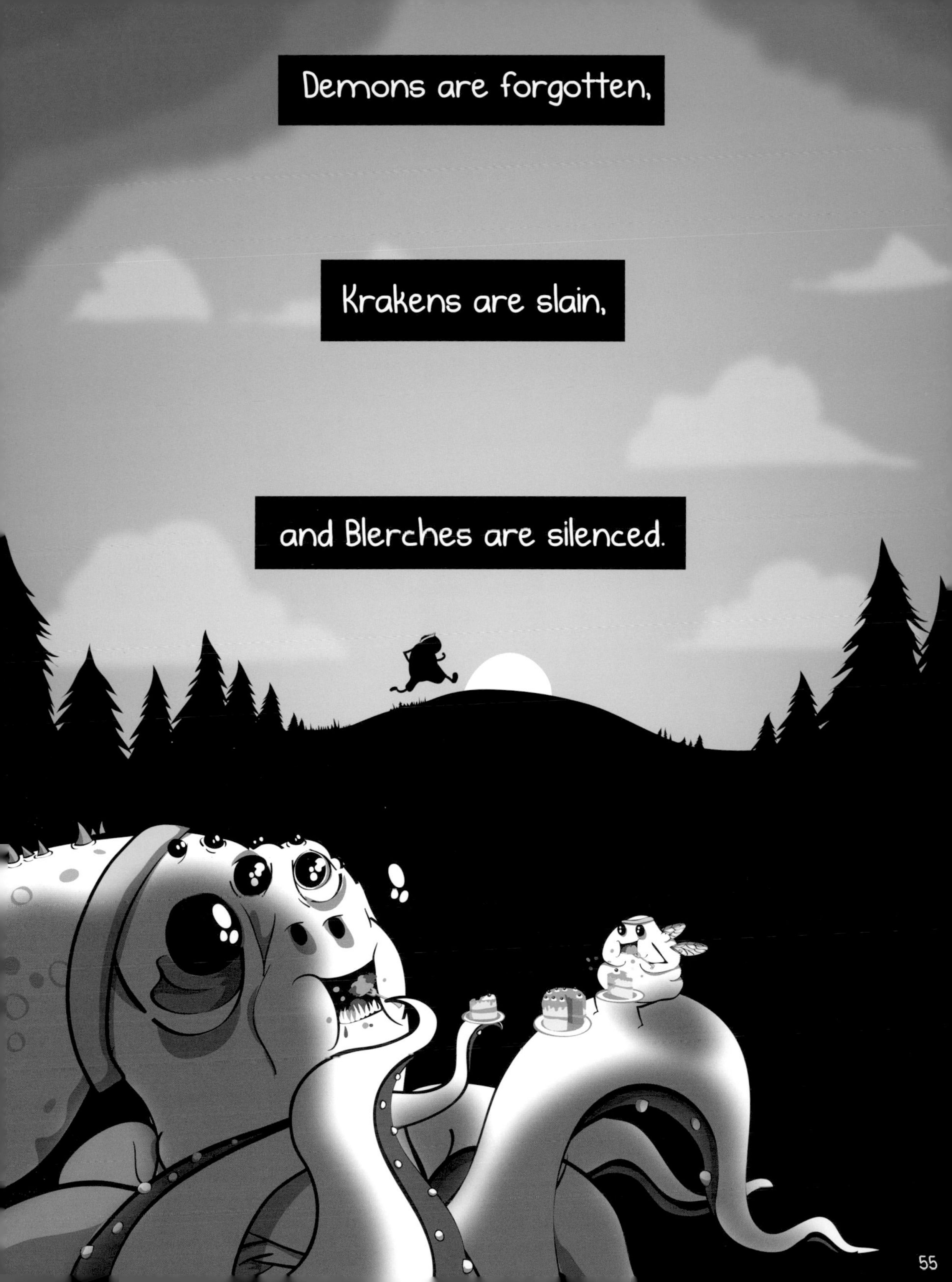
Demons are forgotten,
Krakens are slain,
and Blerches are silenced.

THE END.

In the previous chapter, I mentioned being chased by Japanese giant hornets. For the sake of brevity, I left out a rather interesting tidbit about the dynamic that exists between these awful hornets and their not-nearly-so-awful cousin:

the Japanese honeybee.

So, in the name of science, I am happy to present:

A TOTALLY UNNECESSARY DIGRESSION ABOUT

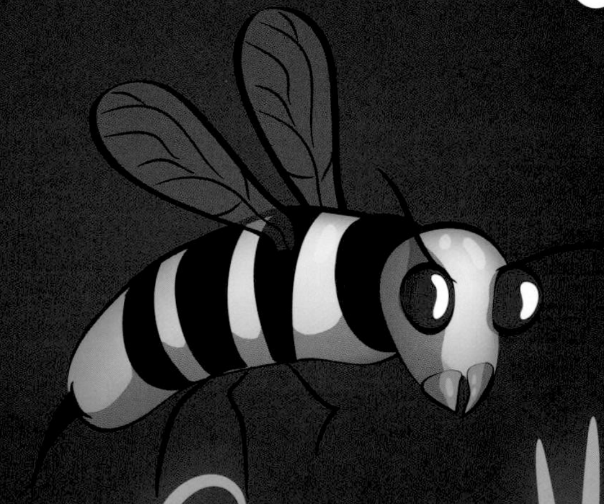

JAPANESE GIANT HORNETS

When European honeybees are exposed to Japanese giant hornets, it does not end well for the bees.

A single Japanese giant hornet can kill an average of forty European honeybees a minute,

→ (That's one corpse every 1.5 seconds.)

and a group of thirty can wipe out a colony of 10,000 European honeybees in an **hour**.

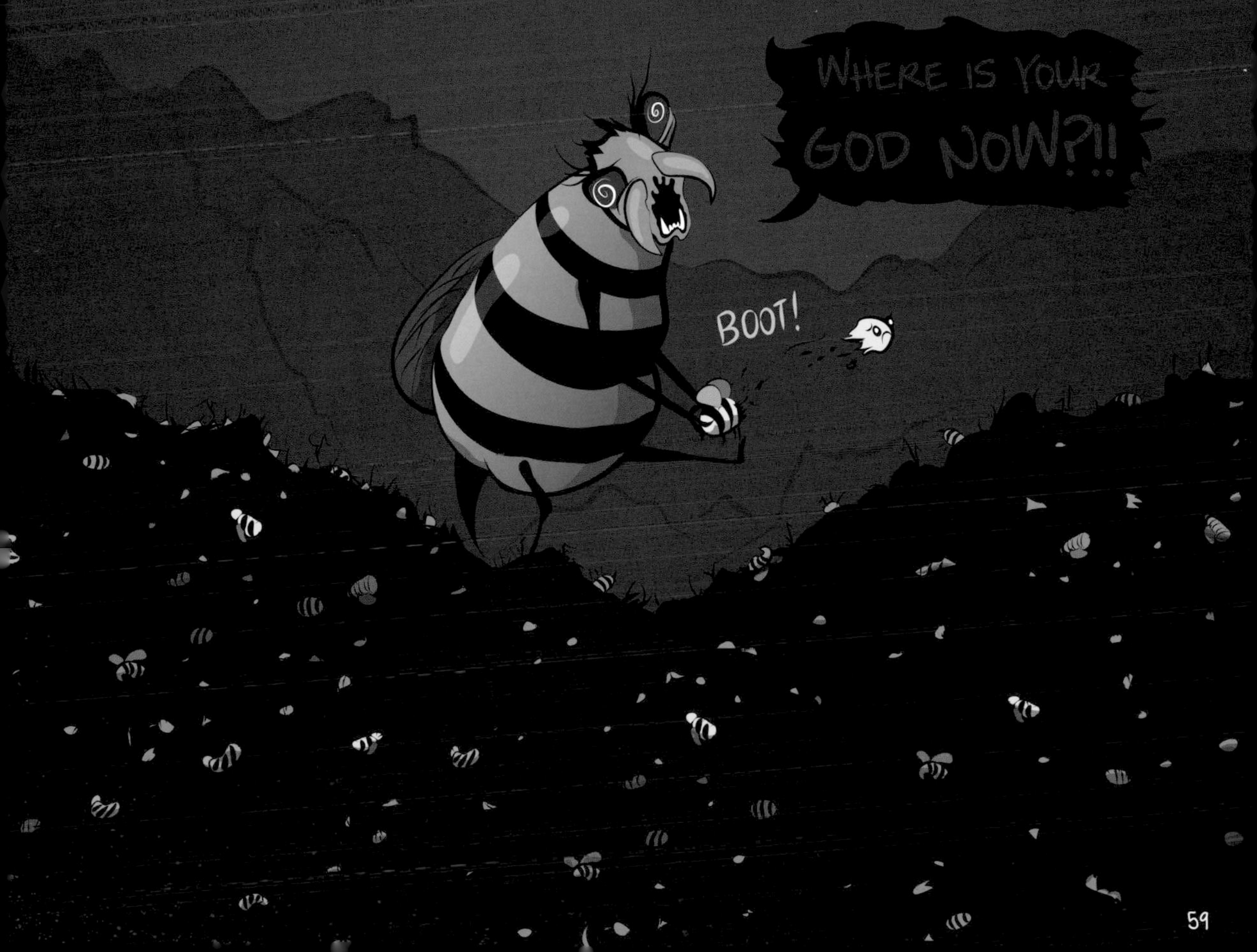
WHERE IS YOUR GOD NOW?!!
BOOT!

This is because European honeybees did not evolve alongside Japanese hornets, and therefore have no natural defense against them. *Japanese* honeybees, however, have had OCEANS of time to deal with these flesh-melting, nightmarish creatures, and have evolved a very unique way of combating them.

When a hornet nears their nest, Japanese honeybees will swarm the hornet and enclose it in a tight ball.

HUG!
HUG LIKE

The honeybees will then vibrate their wings, which turns the "bee ball" into a convection oven.

BZZ
BZZ
COMMENCE OPERATION
STEAMY HOT

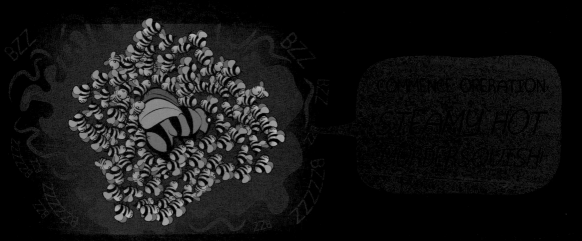

Japanese honeybees can survive in temperatures of up to 122°F (50 C), but a Japanese giant hornet can only withstand temperatures of up to 115°F (46 C).

So, the honeybees will raise the internal temperature of the ball to exactly 117°F (47 C),

Hornet
neybees

110F   115F   120F   125F

thereby roasting the hornet to death,
but leaving themselves unscathed.

B-DAY

Isn't nature neat?

of running your first

MARATHON.

DO let those pre-race jitters fly!

Start out at a completely impractical pace. This will demoralize other runners into quitting early, and you will be crowned marathon champion at mile two.

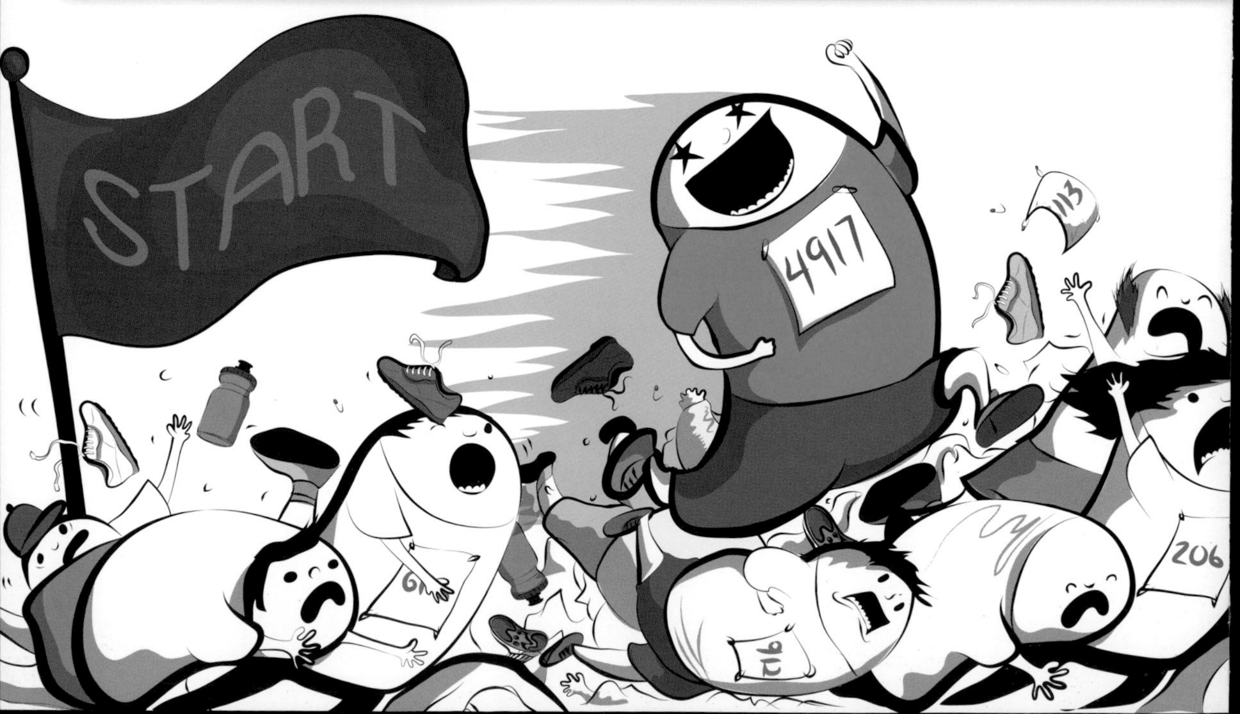

START
4917
113
206

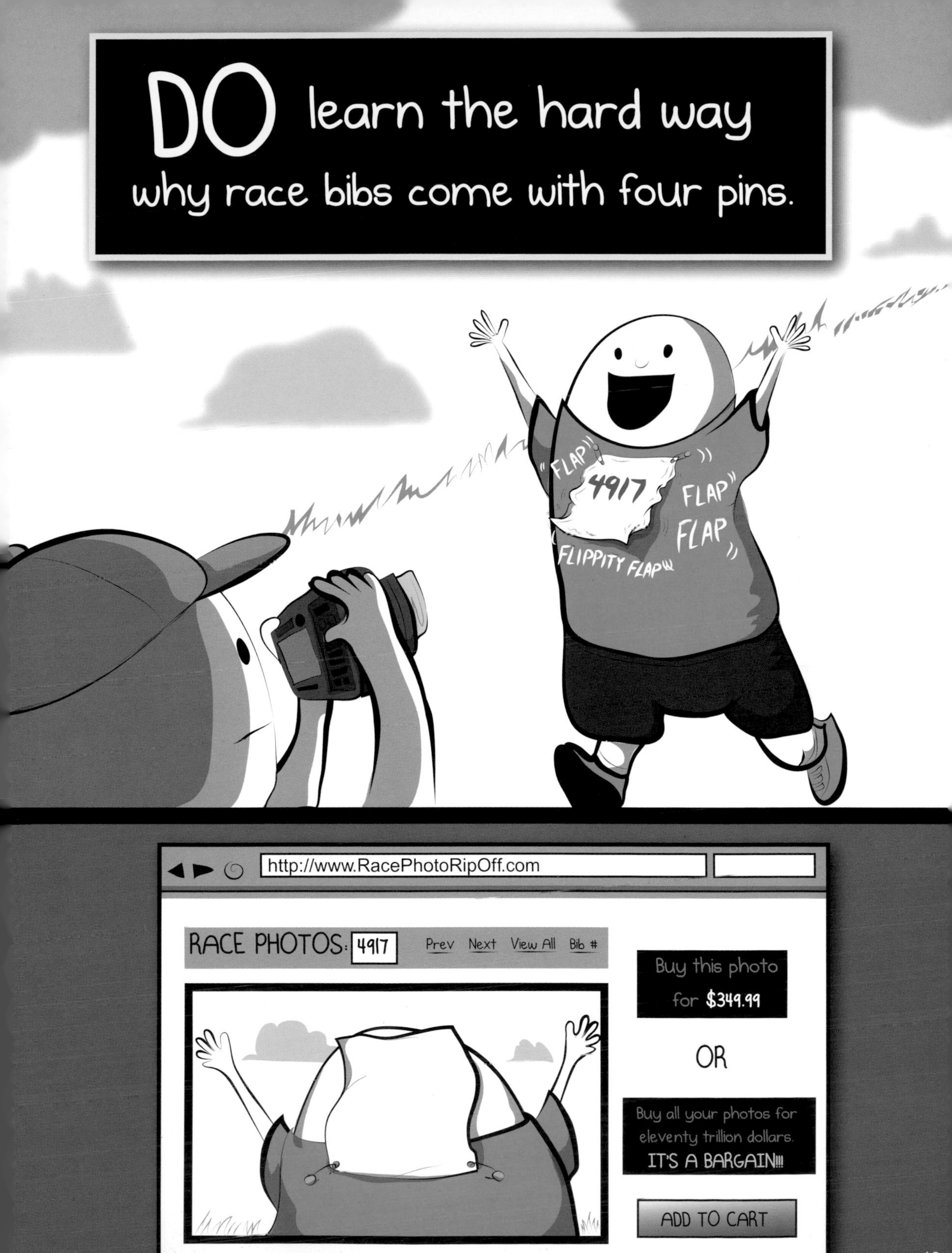
DO learn the hard way
why race bibs come with four pins.
FLAP
4917
FLAP
FLAP
FLIPPITY FLAP
http://www.RacePhotoRipOff.com
RACE PHOTOS: 4917
Prev Next View All Bib #
Buy this photo for $349.99
OR
Buy all your photos for eleventy trillion dollars. IT'S A BARGAIN!!!
ADD TO CART

DO NOT stop running when getting a drink at an aid station.

By enduring the "sprint-choke," you could shave three, possibly four seconds off your 5+ hour finish time!

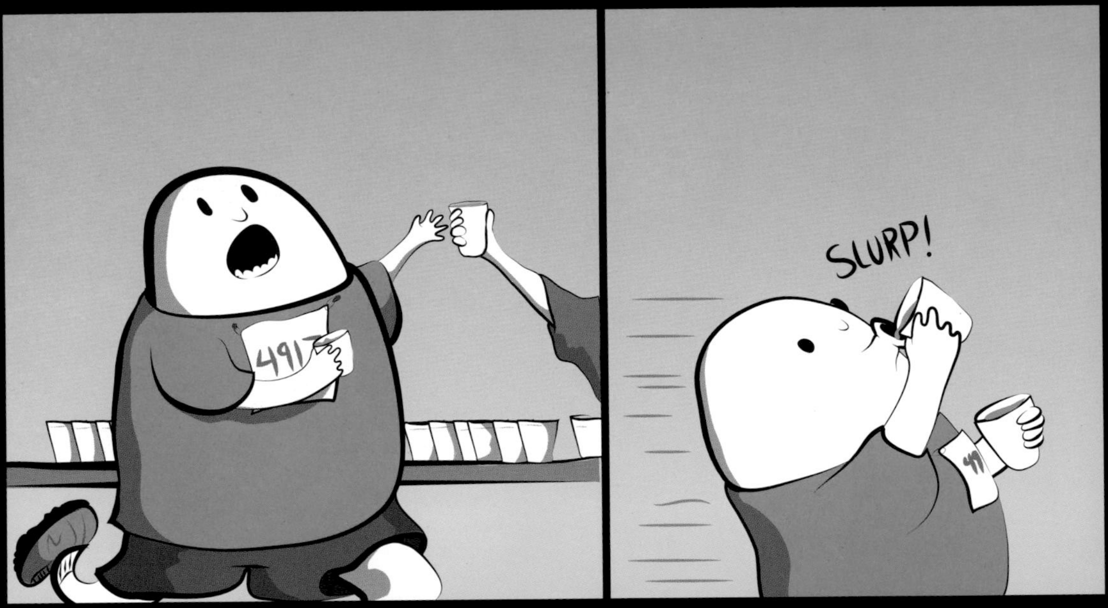
491
SLURP!
491

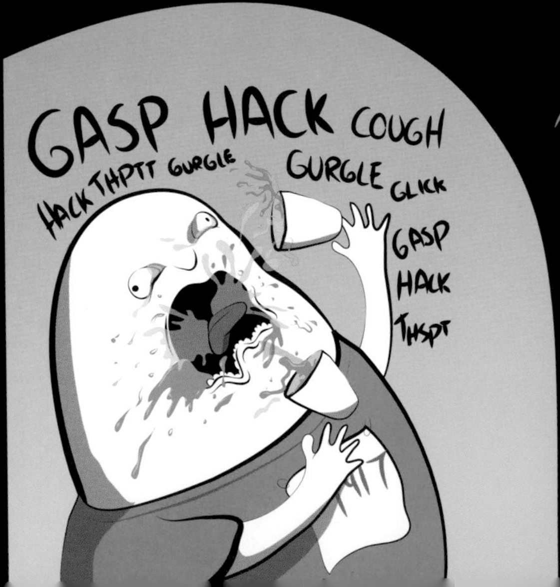
GASP HACK COUGH
HACK THPTT GURGLE
GURGLE GLICK
GASP
HACK
THSPT

Remember:

marathon success does not com
from training or perseverance,
it comes from waterboarding
yourself at aid stations.

DO delude yourself
into thinking there is anything enjoyable about eating energy gels.
This tastes like boob milk from a cyborg.
And how!

DO enjoy massive surges of adrenaline

and find yourself laughing really hard at things that aren't actually that funny ...

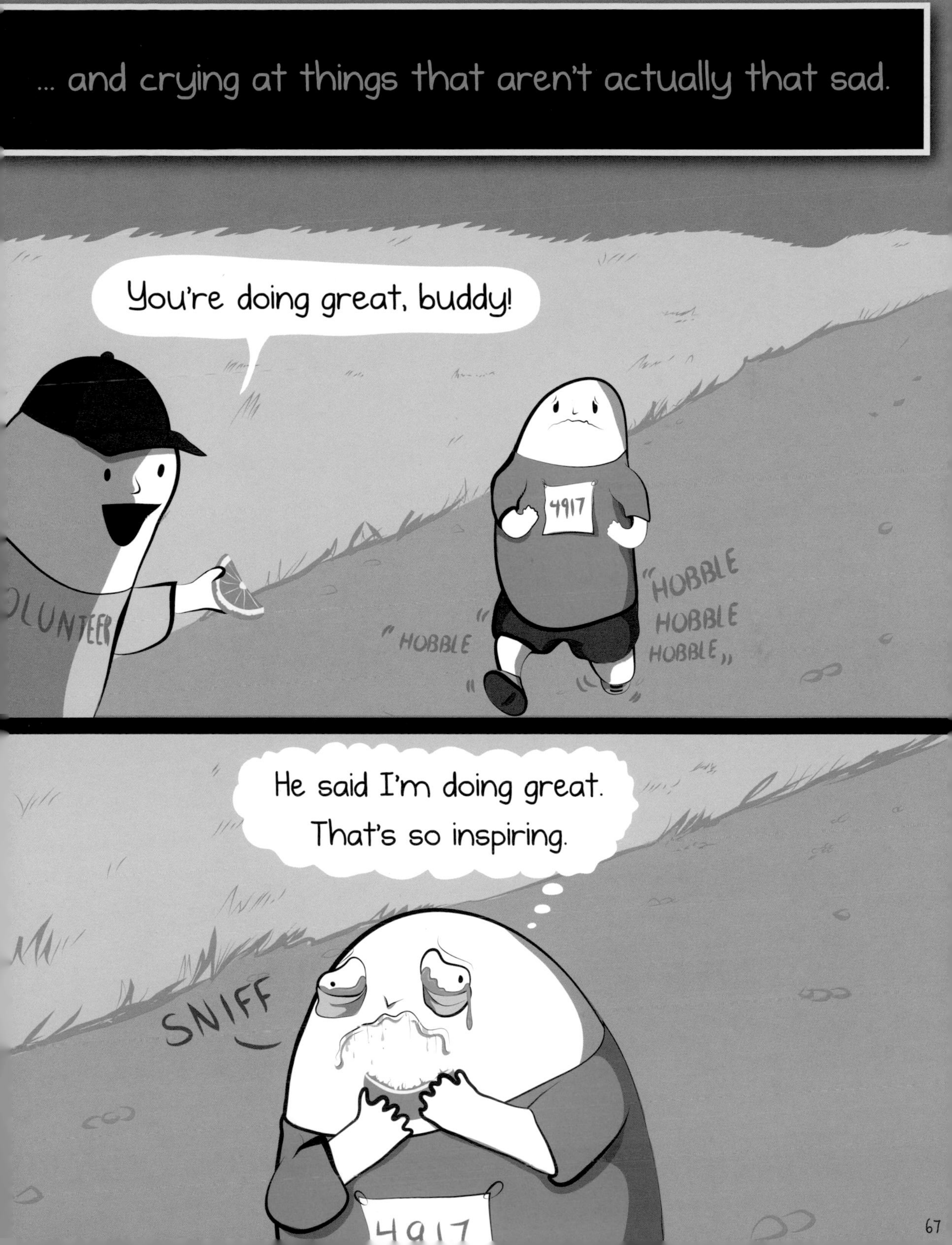
... and crying at things that aren't actually that sad.
You're doing great, buddy!
VOLUNTEER
4917
"HOBBLE
HOBBLE
HOBBLE
HOBBLE"
He said I'm doing great. That's so inspiring.
SNIFF
4917

DO over-accessorize.

Because you're totally gonna need all that shit.

DO NOT dwell on those who are clearly doing much better than you are.

For they will only drain your life force.

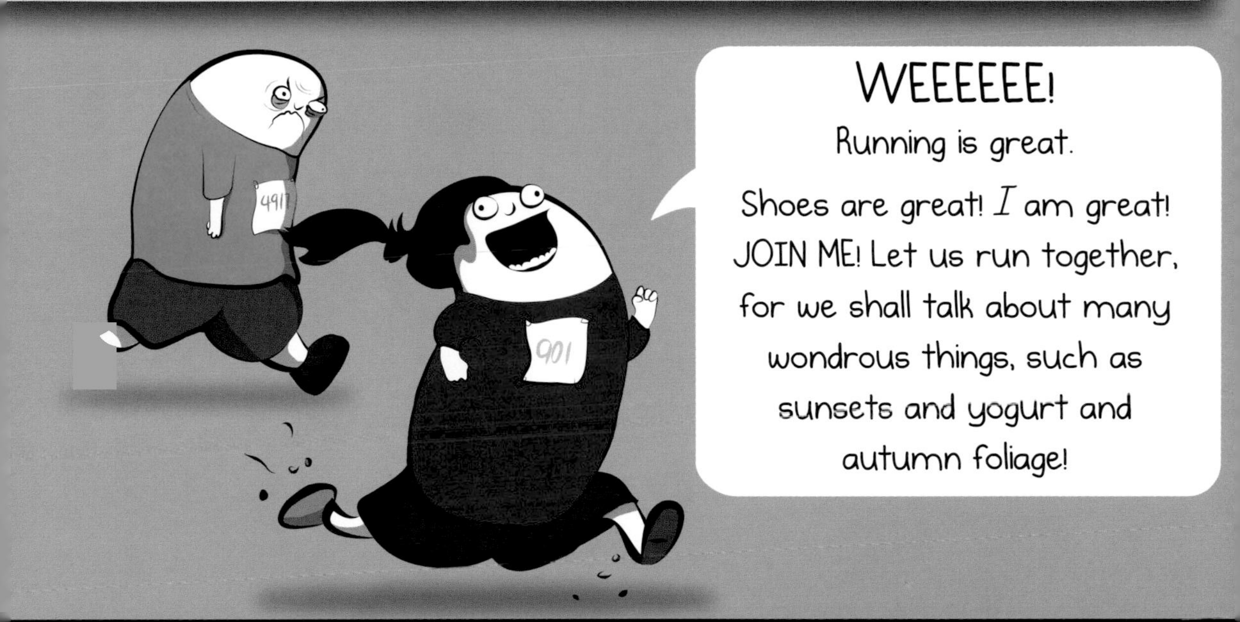
WEEEEEE!
Running is great.
Shoes are great! *I* am great! JOIN ME! Let us run together, for we shall talk about many wondrous things, such as sunsets and yogurt and autumn foliage!
4917
901

INSTEAD focus on those who are clearly in hell.

I call these people "springboards."

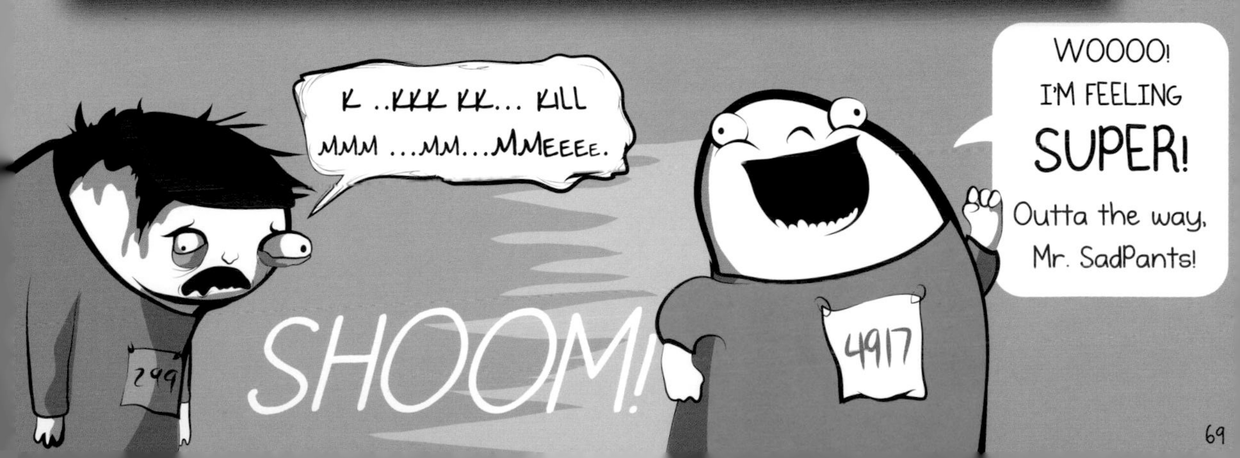
K ..KKK KK... KILL MMM ...MM...MMEEEE.
WOOOO!
I'M FEELING
SUPER!
Outta the way, Mr. SadPants!
SHOOM!
249
4917

DO NOT remind yourself that you paid good money for this.

---

marathon: *(noun)*

A popular form of overpriced torture wherein participants wake up at ass-o-clock in the morning and stand in the freezing cold until it's time to run, at which point they miserably trot for a god-awful interval of time that could be better spent sleeping in and/or consuming large quantities of beer and cupcakes.

See also: masochism, awfulness, "a bunch of bullshit," boob-chafing, cupcake deprivation therapy.

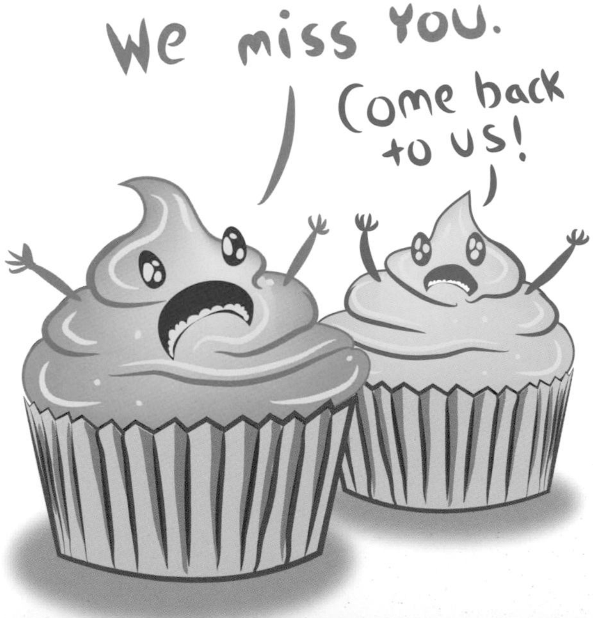
We miss you.
Come back to us!

DO NOT despair

when thinking about how much farther you have to go.

Instead, console yourself by inventing bizarre ways of measuring distances.

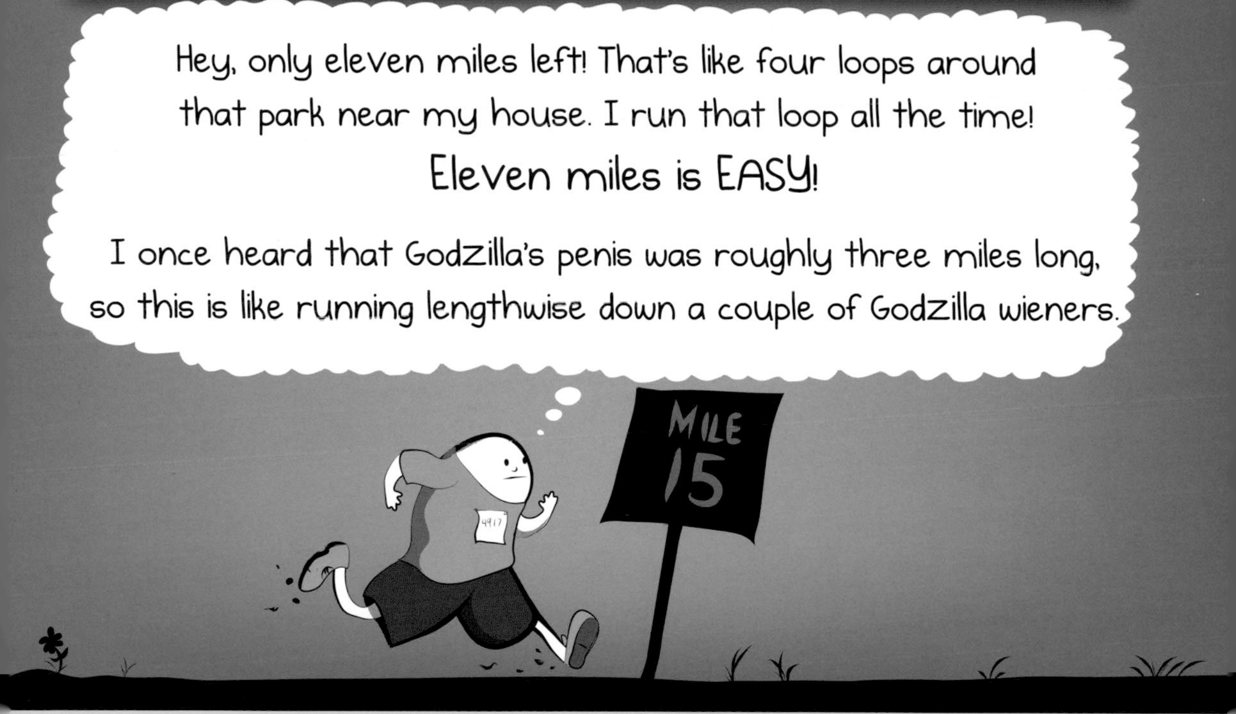

Hey, only eleven miles left! That's like four loops around that park near my house. I run that loop all the time!
Eleven miles is EASY!
I once heard that Godzilla's penis was roughly three miles long, so this is like running lengthwise down a couple of Godzilla wieners.
MILE 15
4917

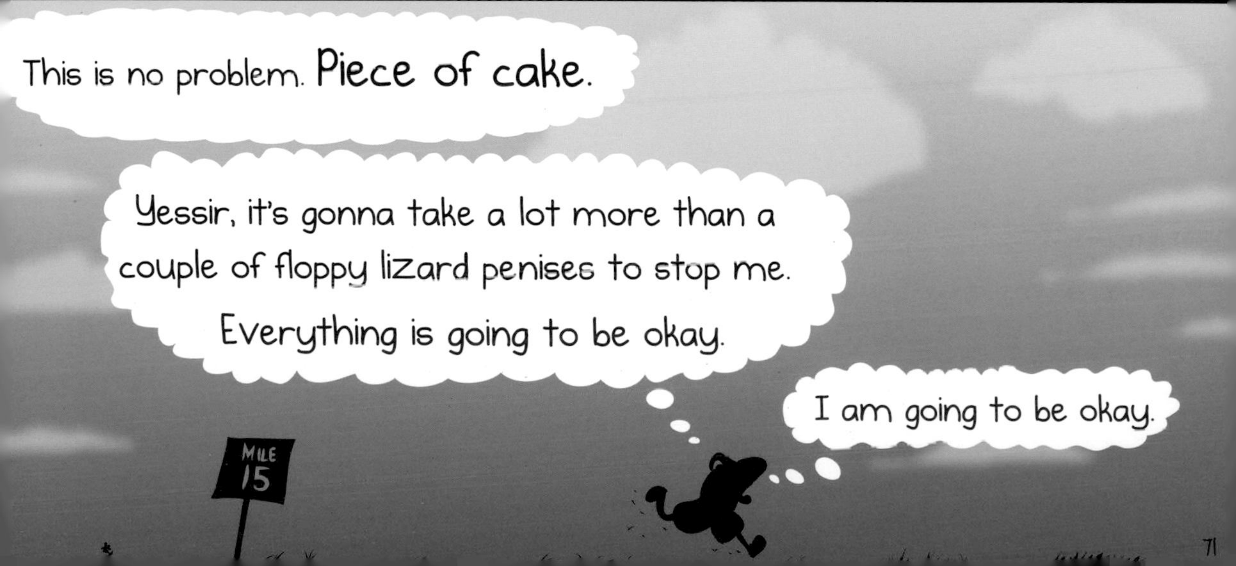

This is no problem. Piece of cake.
Yessir, it's gonna take a lot more than a couple of floppy lizard penises to stop me.
Everything is going to be okay.
I am going to be okay.
MILE 15

DO end on a high note.

When you see the finish line,
start sprinting like a coked-out orangutan.

No one will ever suspect that you walk-jogged the previous 26 miles.

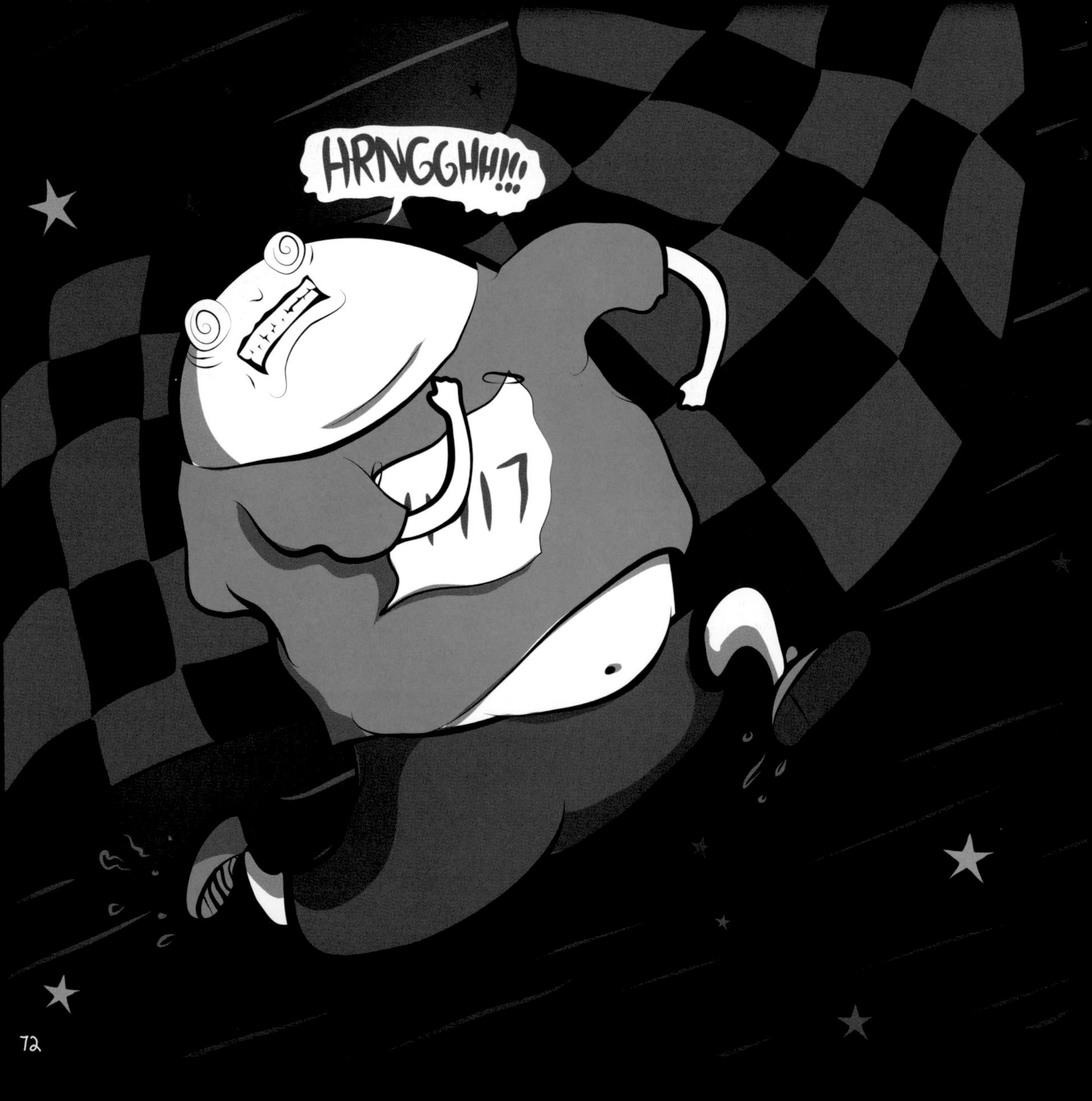
HRNGGHH!!!
117

✓ **DO** hang out in the recovery area and chat up the happiest bunch of physically battered people you'll ever meet.

✓ **DO** ignore all the warning signs that something horribly traumatic has just happened to your body.

✓ **DO** forget every single second of agony, frustration, and melancholy that plagued you over the past few hours.

✓ **DO** this with food in your face and a gleam in your eye.

✓ **DO** all of these things,

and then go enthusiastically sign up for another race.

Same time next year?

ROGER THAT, GOOD BUDDY.

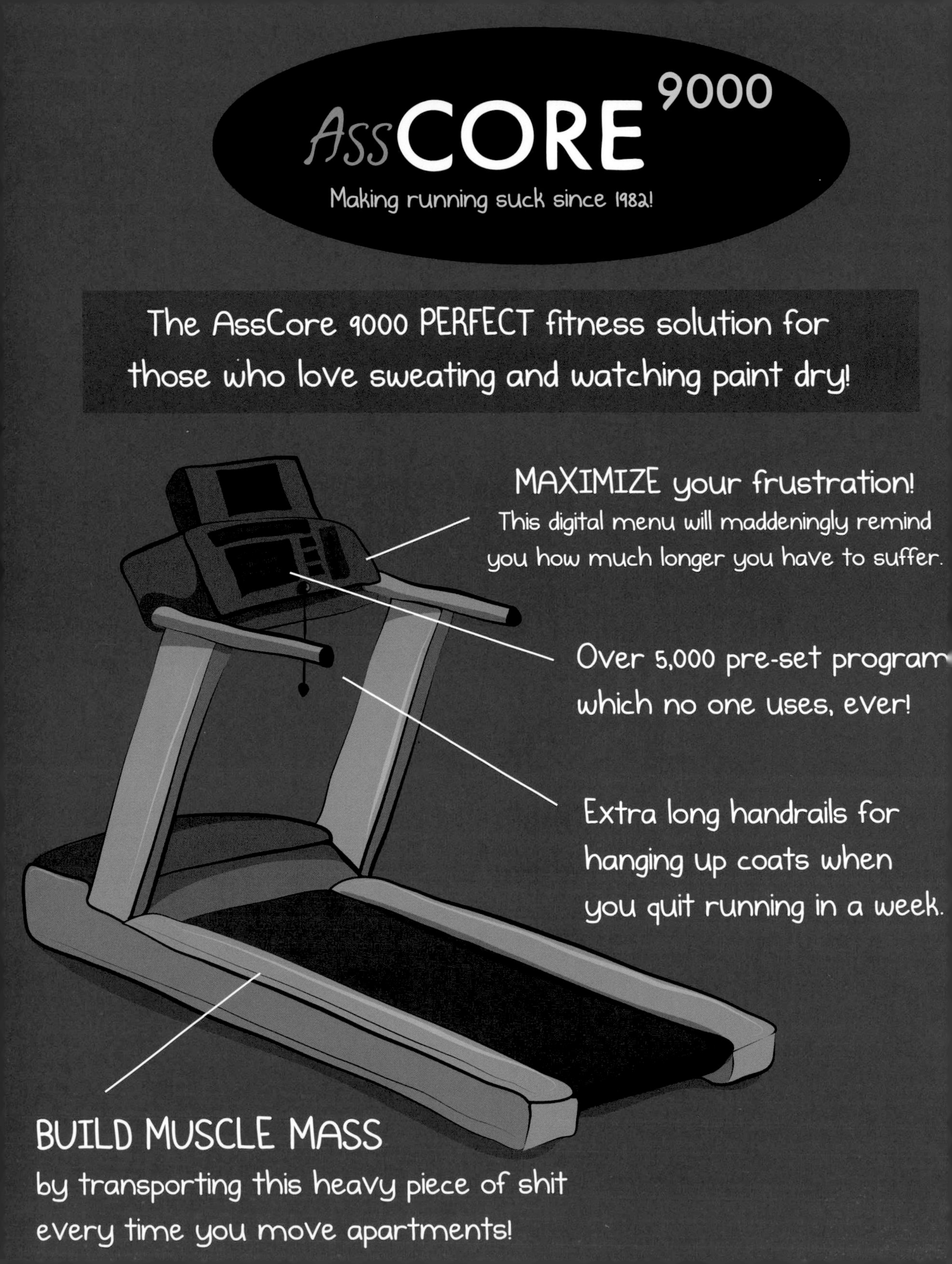

9000
AssCORE
Making running suck since 1982!
The AssCore 9000 PERFECT fitness solution for those who love sweating and watching paint dry!
MAXIMIZE your frustration!
This digital menu will maddeningly remind you how much longer you have to suffer.
Over 5,000 pre-set program which no one uses, ever!
Extra long handrails for hanging up coats when you quit running in a week.
BUILD MUSCLE MASS
by transporting this heavy piece of shit every time you move apartments!

Hate the outdoors?

SO DO WE!

There are beavers and pine cones
and a bunch of other crazy bullshit.

With the AssCore 9000,
you can safely exercise indoors
while catching up on bad television!

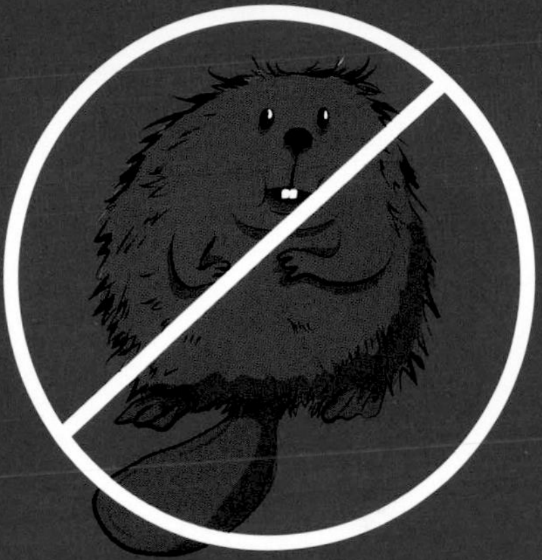

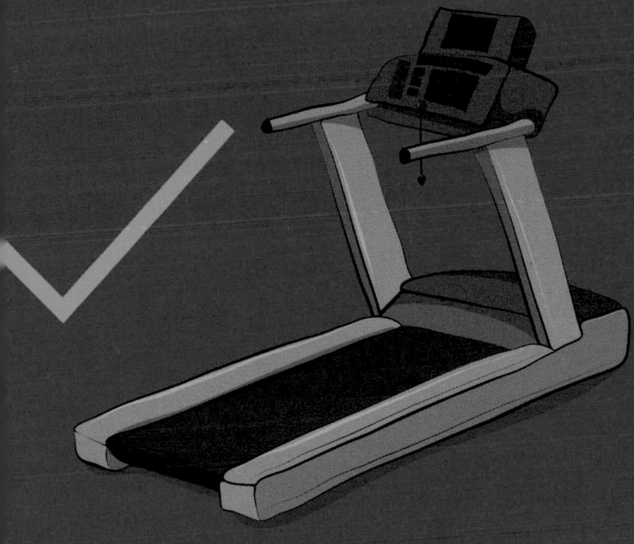

100% fewer beavers,
pine cones, and
life experiences,
<u>GUARANTEED!</u>

ORDER NOW

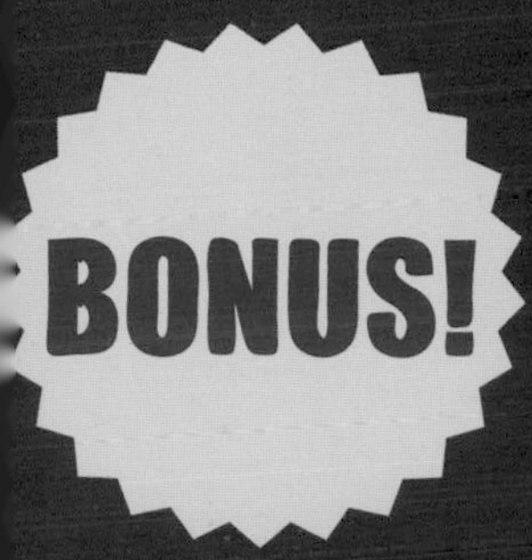
BONUS!

and we'll throw in a FREE
DVD featuring 14 hours of
gerbils running in
elliptical patterns.

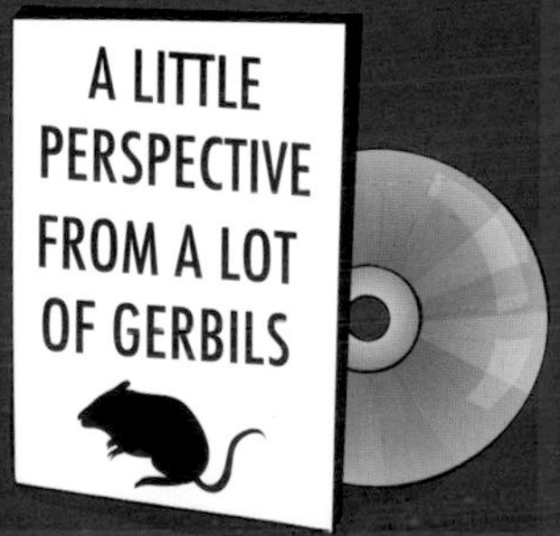
A LITTLE PERSPECTIVE FROM A LOT OF GERBILS

The Blerch's guide to dieting.

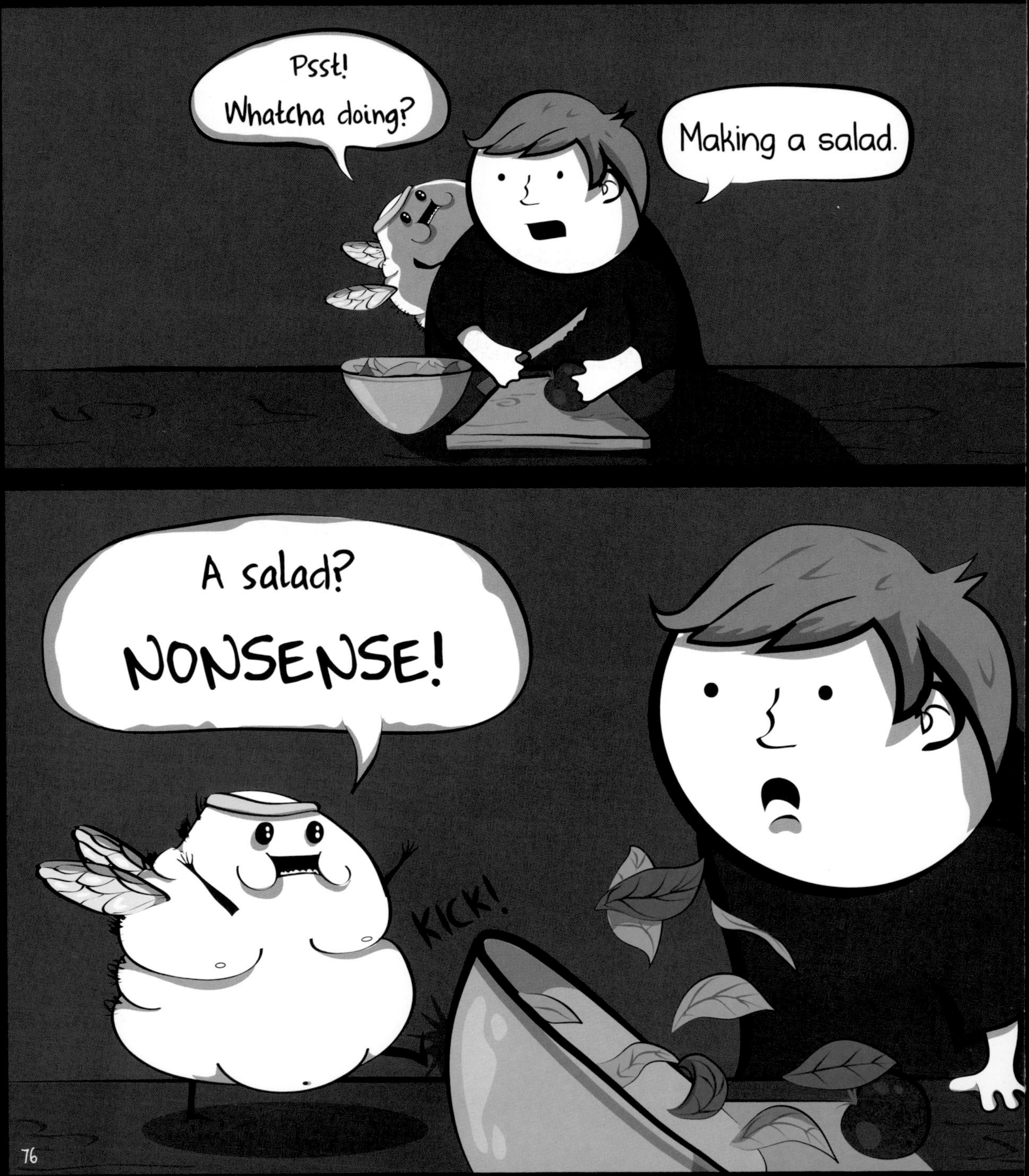
Psst!
Whatcha doing?
Making a salad.
A salad?
NONSENSE!
KICK!

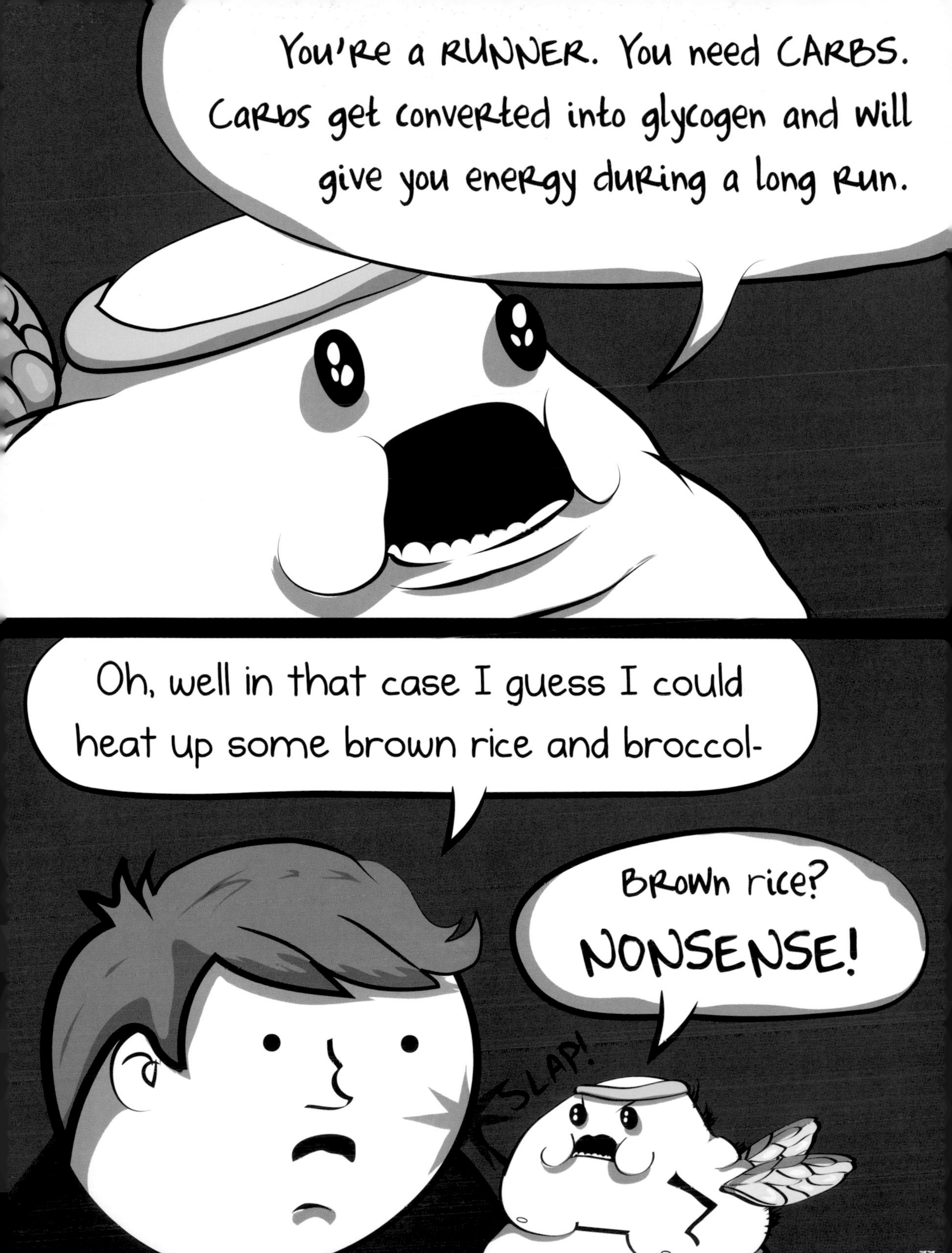
You're a RUNNER. You need CARBS. Carbs get converted into glycogen and will give you energy during a long run.
Oh, well in that case I guess I could heat up some brown rice and broccol-
Brown rice? NONSENSE!
SLAP!

You're a RUNNER. You need high-calorie foods! Endurance athletes like yourself have a massive calorie deficit to make up for!
Well, I suppose I should eat these bear claws then.

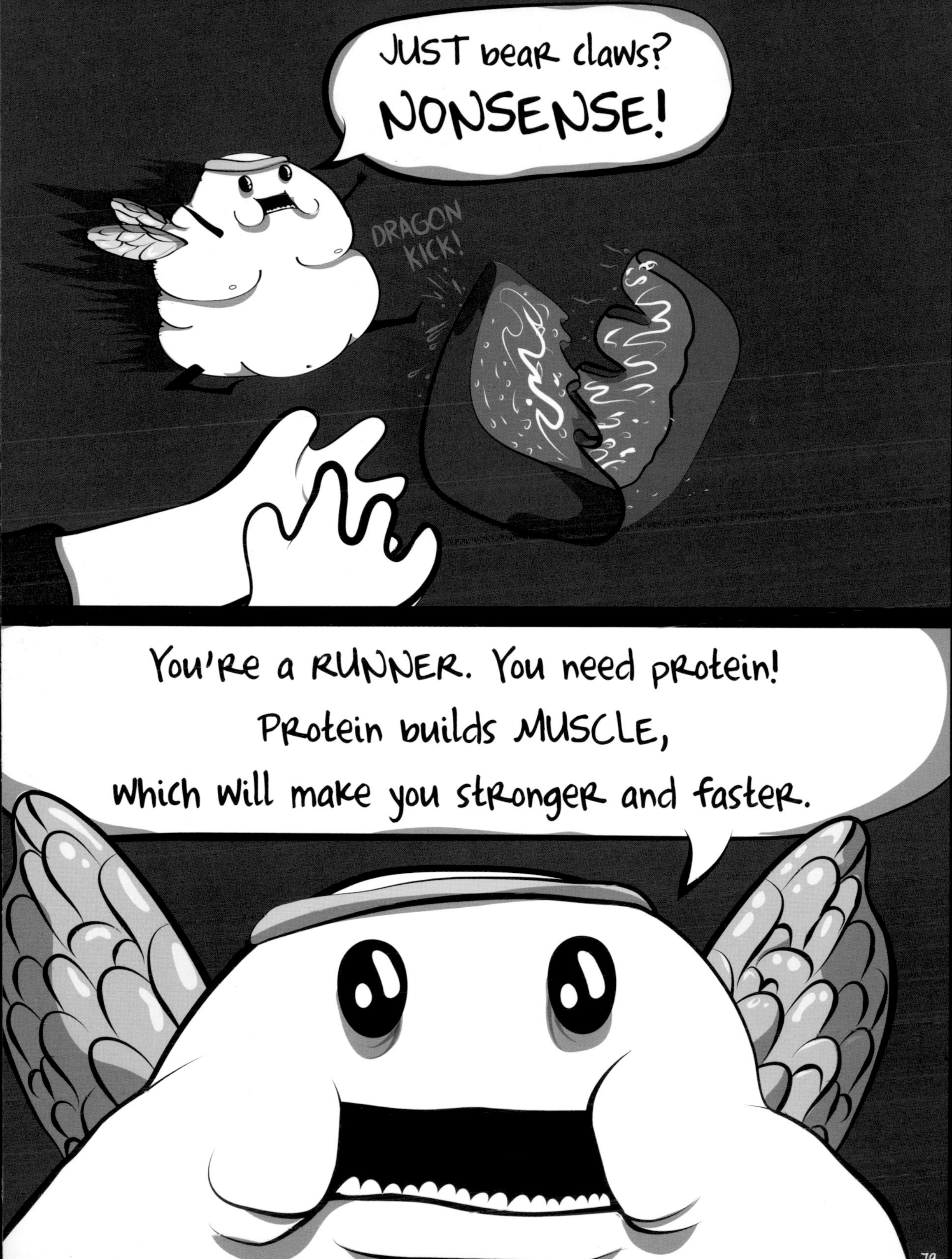
JUST bear claws?
NONSENSE!
DRAGON KICK!
You're a RUNNER. You need protein! Protein builds MUSCLE, which will make you stronger and faster.

I'll cover them in cheese then. Cheese is high in protein.
EZ CHEESE
FSSHHH!
JUST cheese? NONSENSE!
TOSS!

You're a RUNNER, you need salt! By consuming sodium-rich foods, you'll prevent your legs from cramping up on race day.
Well, I definitely don't want to cramp up! Bacon it is then!

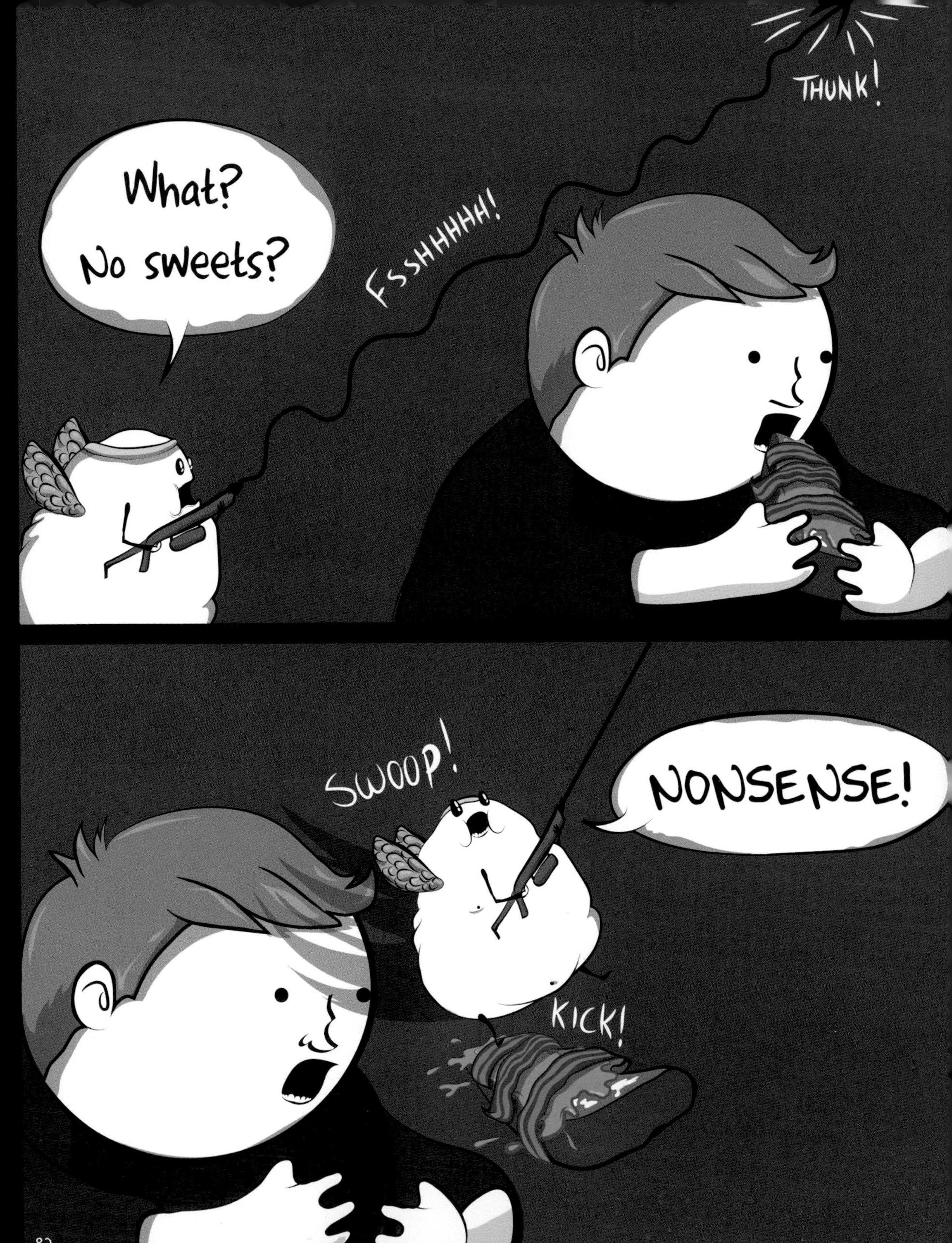
THUNK!
What? No sweets?
FSSHHHHH!
SWOOP!
NONSENSE!
KICK!

You're a runner, you need SUGAR! What do you think is in all those energy gels you eat to keep from bonking?
GUMMY BEARS
Are you sure I should be eating all this stuff?
Eating? NONSENSE! you're fueling!

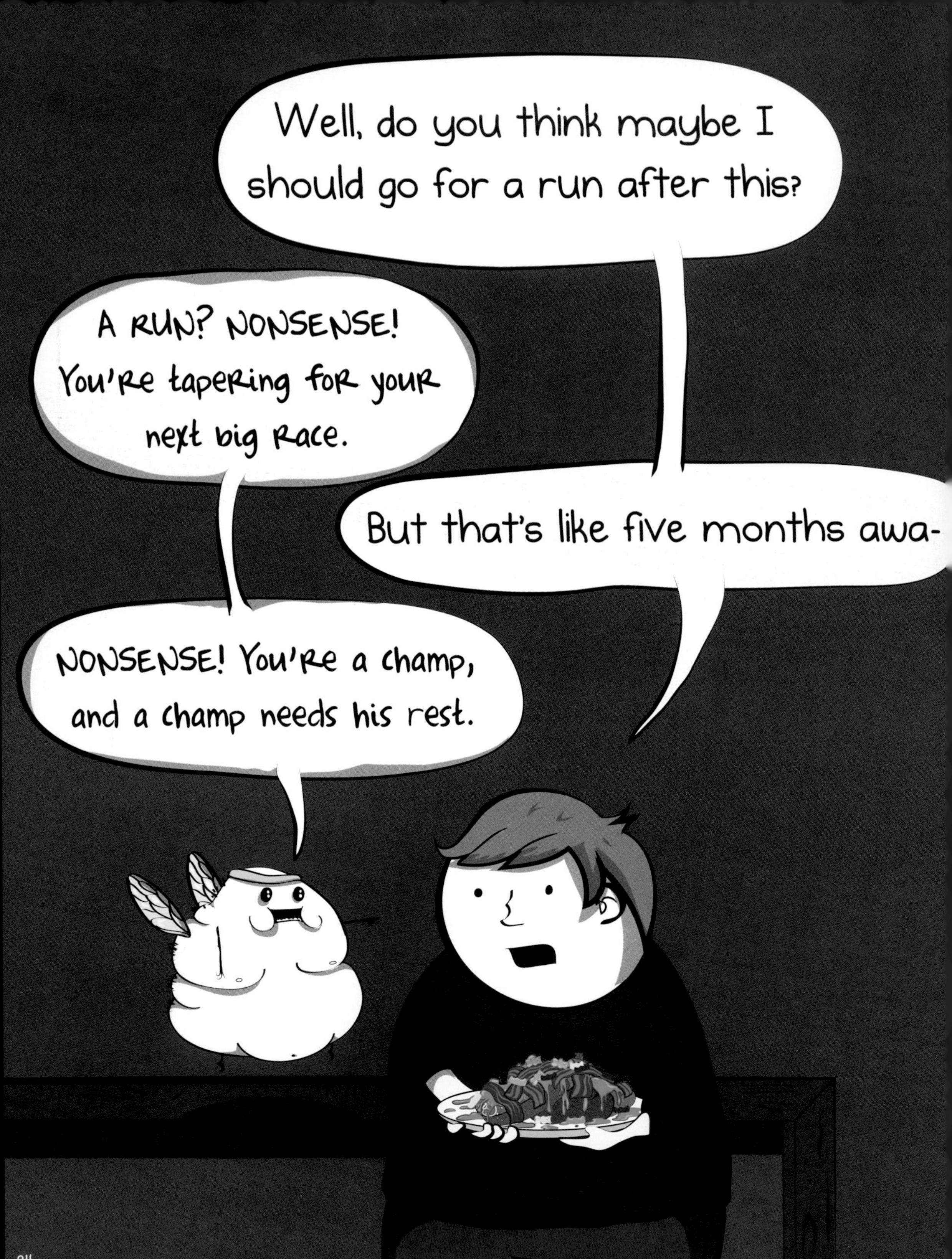
Well, do you think maybe I should go for a run after this?
A RUN? NONSENSE! You're tapering for your next big race.
But that's like five months awa-
NONSENSE! You're a champ, and a champ needs his rest.

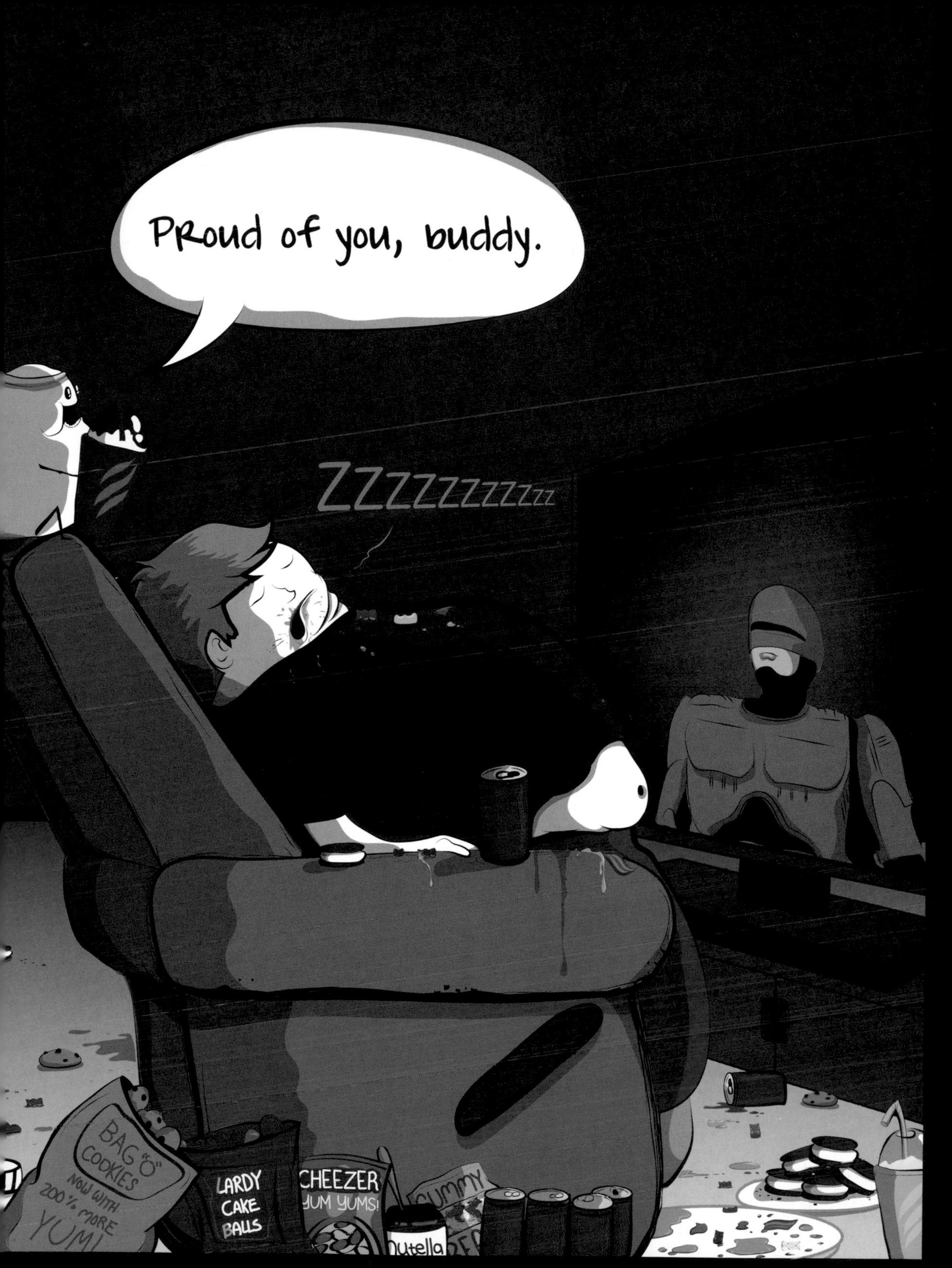
Proud of you, buddy.
ZZZZZZZZZZzz
BAG "O" COOKIES NOW WITH 200% MORE YUM!
LARDY CAKE BALLS
CHEEZER YUM YUMS!
GUMMY
nutella

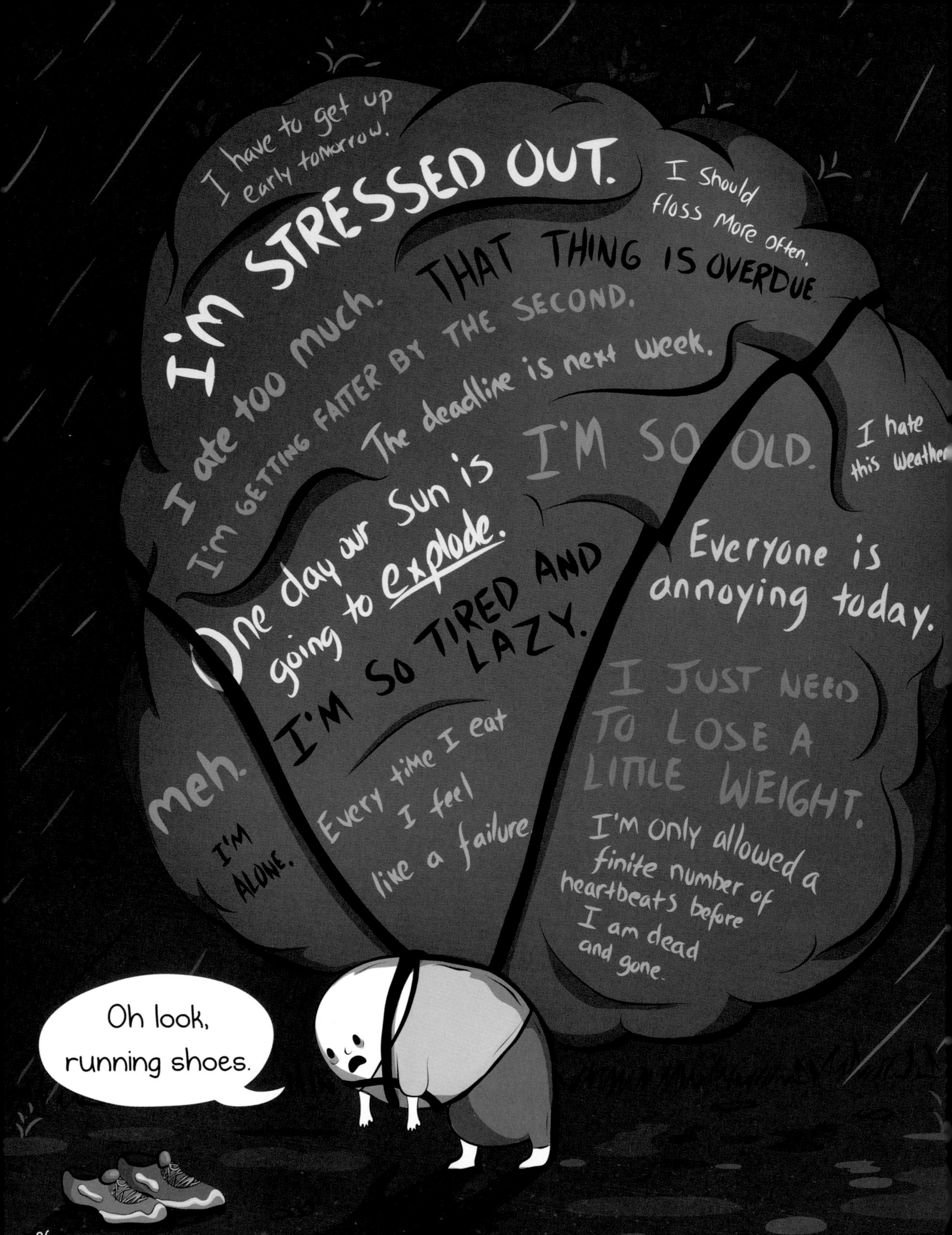
I have to get up early tomorrow.
I'M STRESSED OUT.
I should floss more often.
I ate too much.
THAT THING IS OVERDUE.
I'M GETTING FATTER BY THE SECOND.
The deadline is next week.
I'M SO OLD.
I hate this weather
One day our Sun is going to explode.
I'M SO TIRED AND LAZY.
Everyone is annoying today.
I JUST NEED TO LOSE A LITTLE WEIGHT.
meh.
I'M ALONE.
Every time I eat I feel like a failure.
I'm only allowed a finite number of heartbeats before I am dead and gone.
Oh look, running shoes.

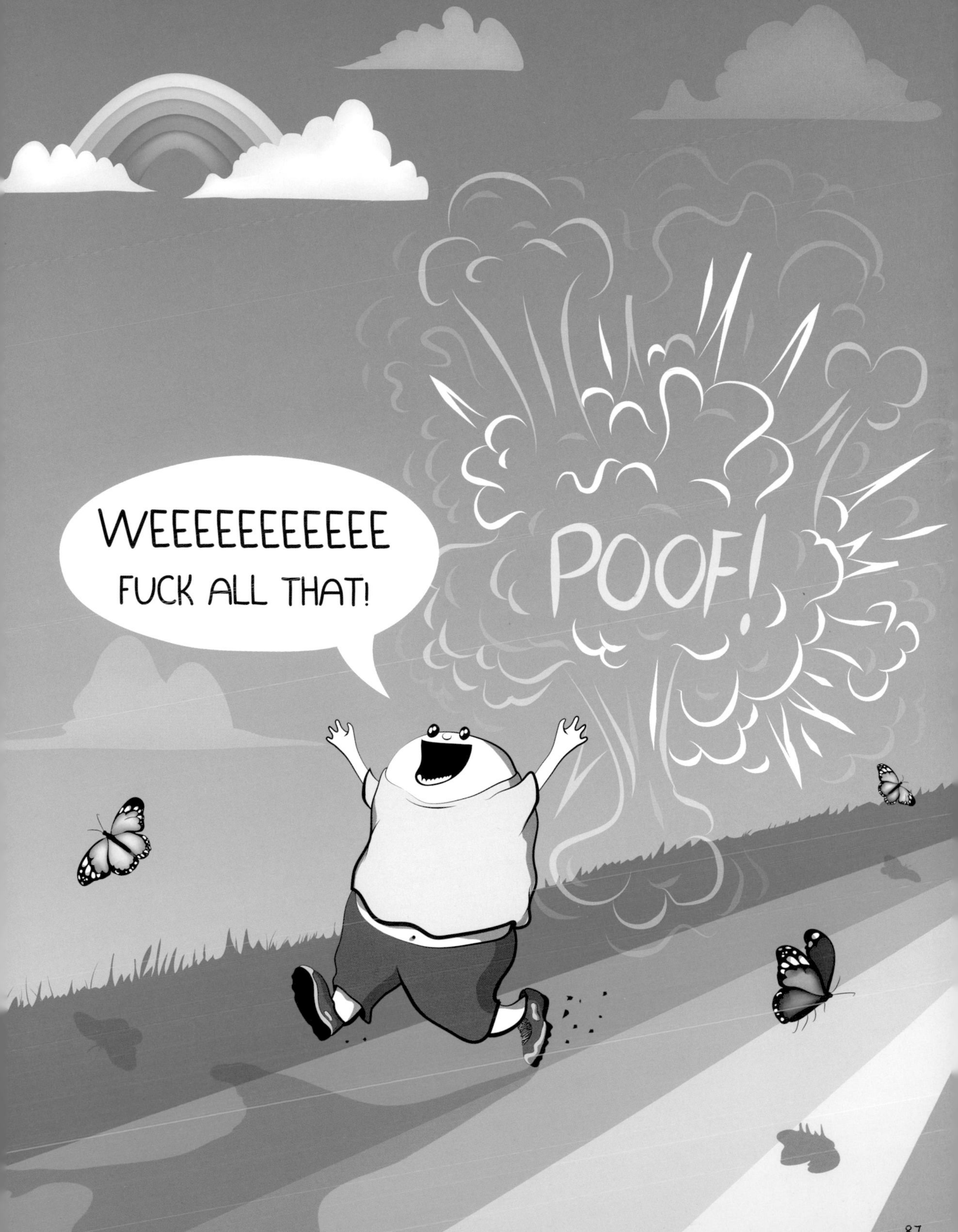
WEEEEEEEEEEE
FUCK ALL THAT!
POOF!

At the gym:

who is looking at whom.

The Large

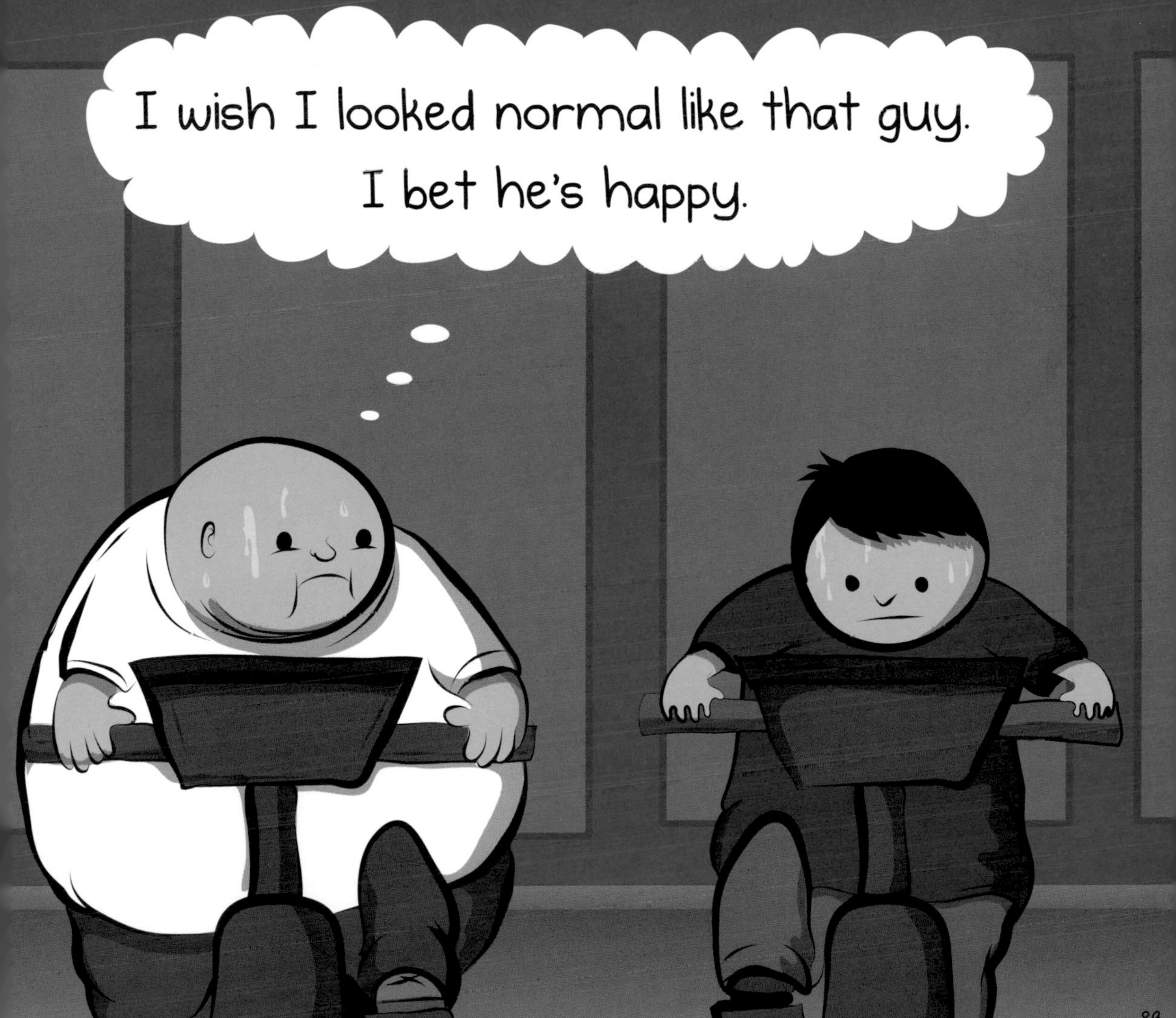
I wish I looked normal like that guy.
I bet he's happy.

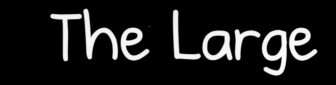

The Normal

I wish I could lose these love handles like that guy. I bet he feels secure.

The Lean

I wish I had gimungus meaty muscles like that guy. I bet girls line up around the block to gargle his privates.

The Meaty
I wish I could say smart, clever things like that guy. I bet people respect him at work.
If I had a nickel for every time a girl told me she wanted to make love to my beard, well ... I'd have a quarter!
hee-hee! It's funny because that's five times.

The Clever

I wish I could walk up to that girl and flirt so perfectly and hilariously that she'd let me motorboat her boobies right here, right now. I bet she wants to talk to me.
Please oh please don't talk to me. I'm here to exercise, not find a mate.

The Boobies
I wish I looked like a starved baked potato like that girl. I bet she feels perfect.

The Starved Baked Potato

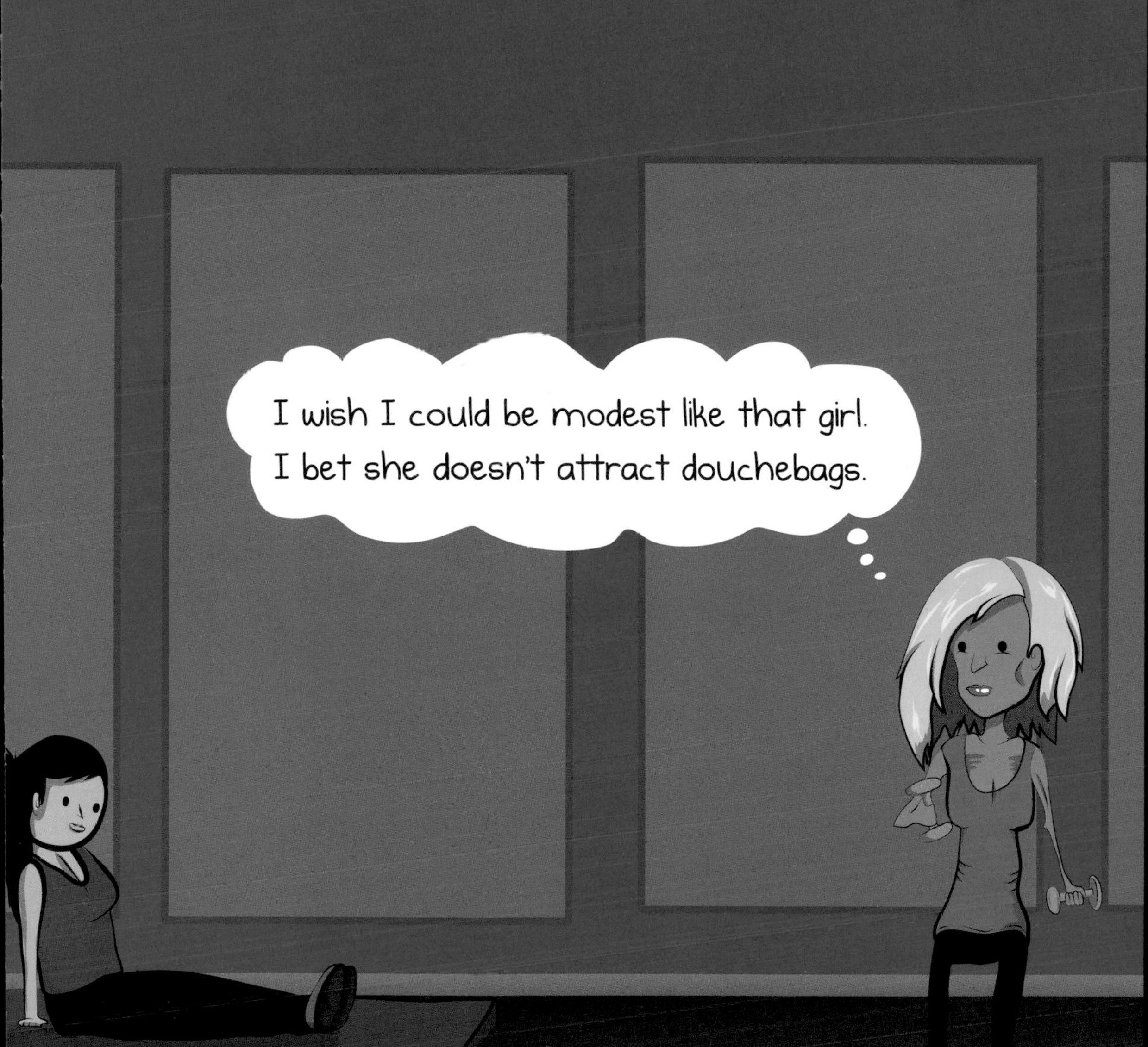

The Elderly
I wish all these vain assholes would stop staring at each other and go the fuck home.
They're all gonna have droopy boobs like me one day, anyway.

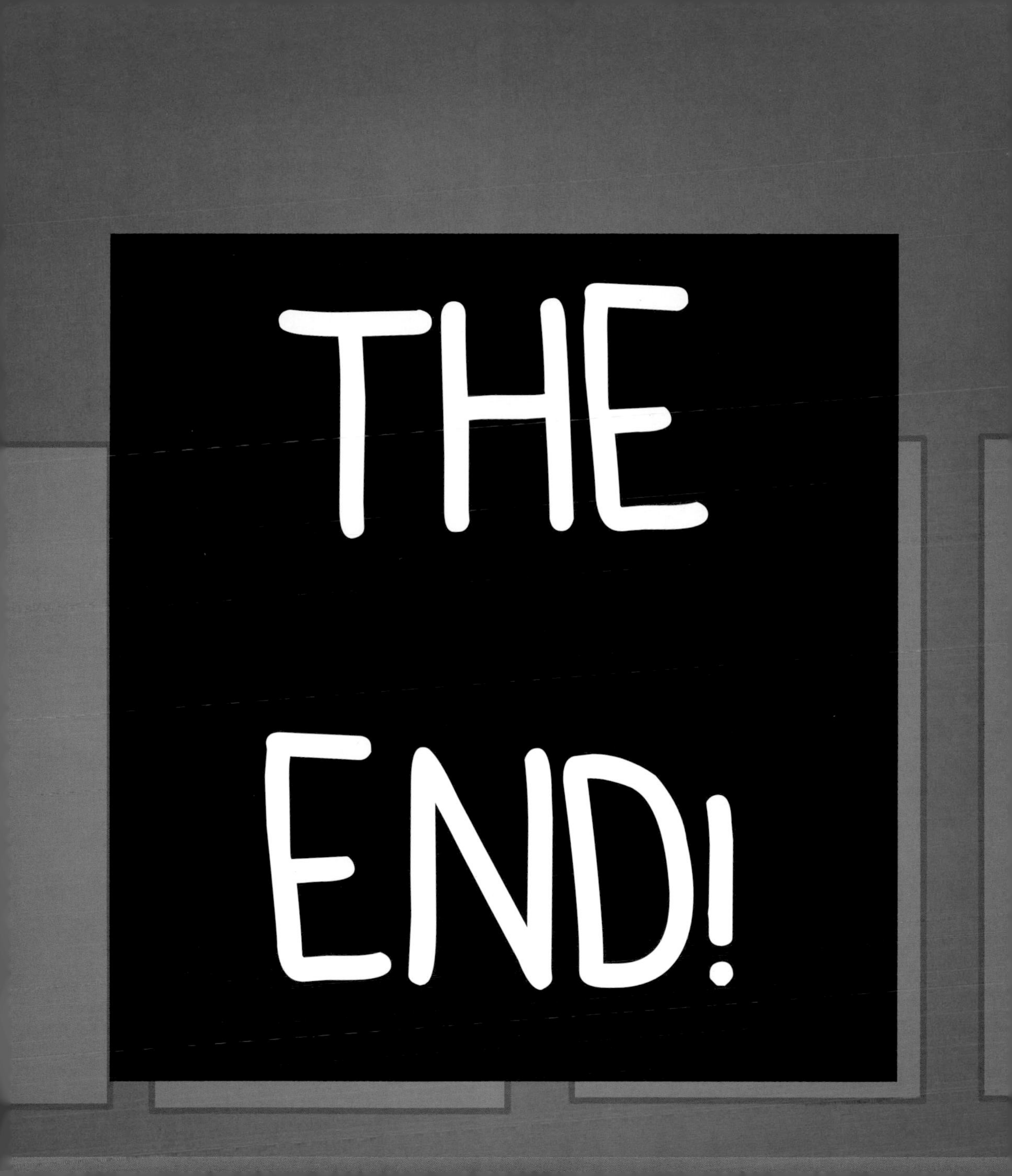
THE END!

LOG OUT,

POWER DOWN,

AND GET THAT SCREEN OUT OF YOUR FACE.

GO OUTDOORS,

EXPERIENCE THE WORLD,

RIGHT NOW.

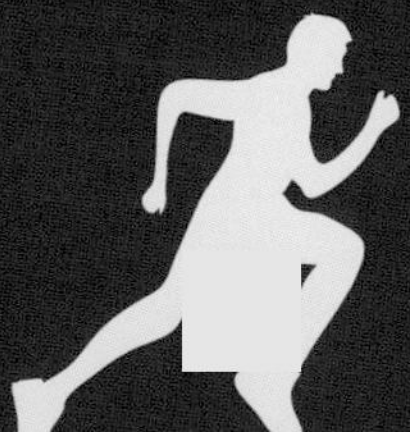

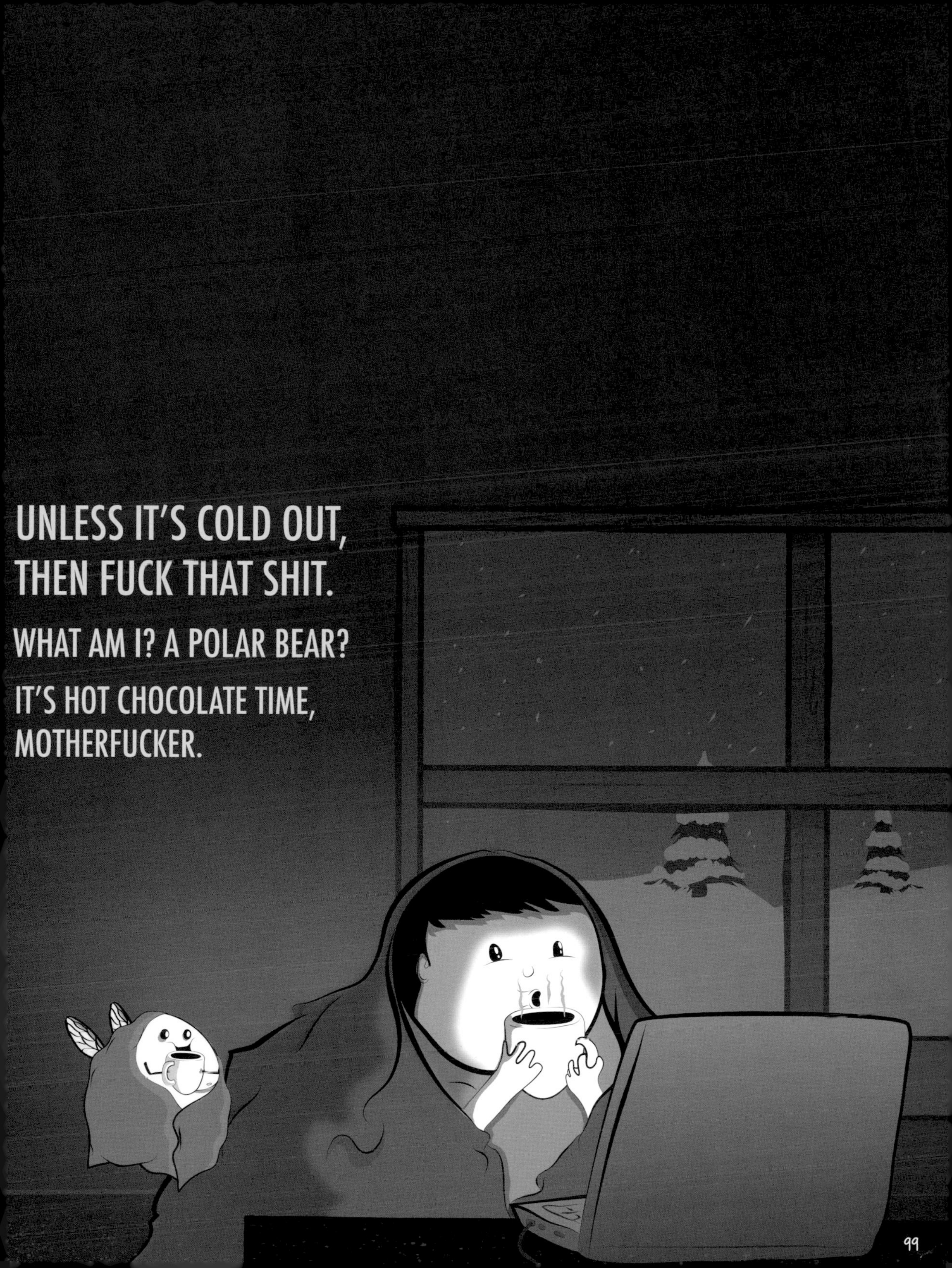
UNLESS IT'S COLD OUT,
THEN FUCK THAT SHIT.
WHAT AM I? A POLAR BEAR?
IT'S HOT CHOCOLATE TIME,
MOTHERFUCKER.

A conversation with my taste buds.

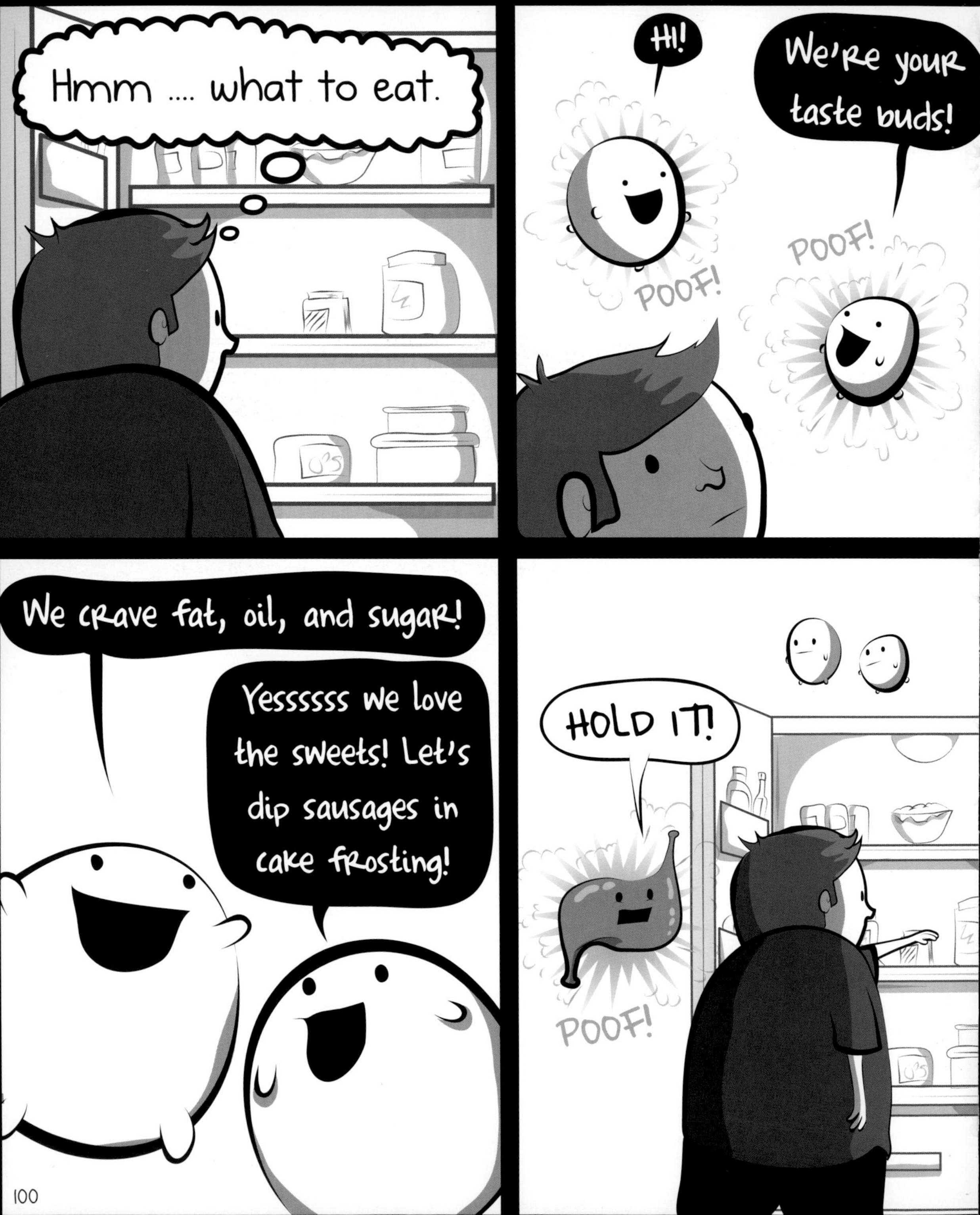
Hmm .... what to eat.
HI!
We're your taste buds!
POOF!
POOF!
We crave fat, oil, and sugar!
Yessssss we love the sweets! Let's dip sausages in cake frosting!
HOLD IT!
POOF!

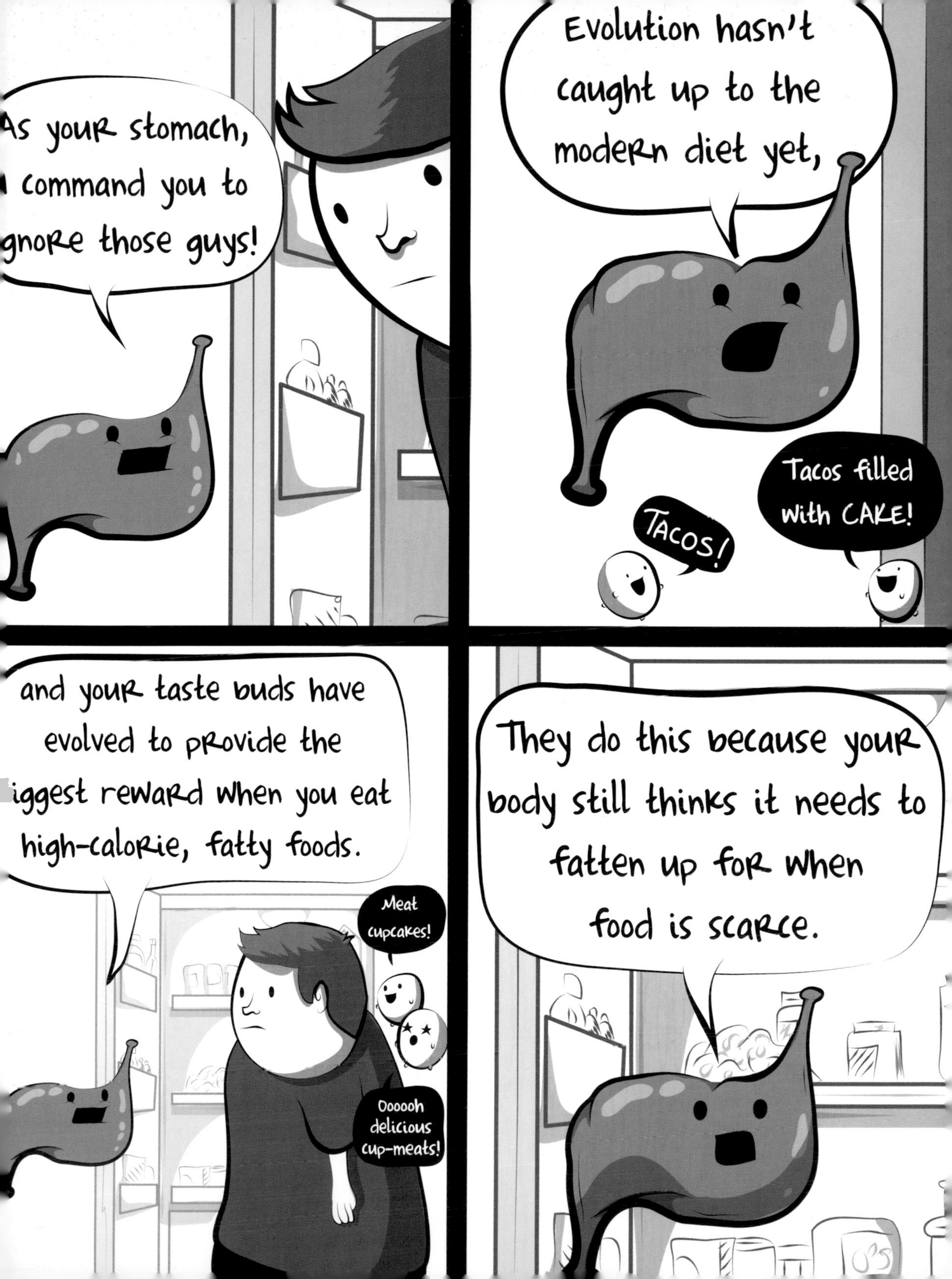
As your stomach, command you to gnore those guys!
Evolution hasn't caught up to the modern diet yet,
TACOS!
Tacos filled with CAKE!
and your taste buds have evolved to provide the iggest reward when you eat high-calorie, fatty foods.
Meat cupcakes!
Oooooh delicious cup-meats!
They do this because your body still thinks it needs to fatten up for when food is scarce.

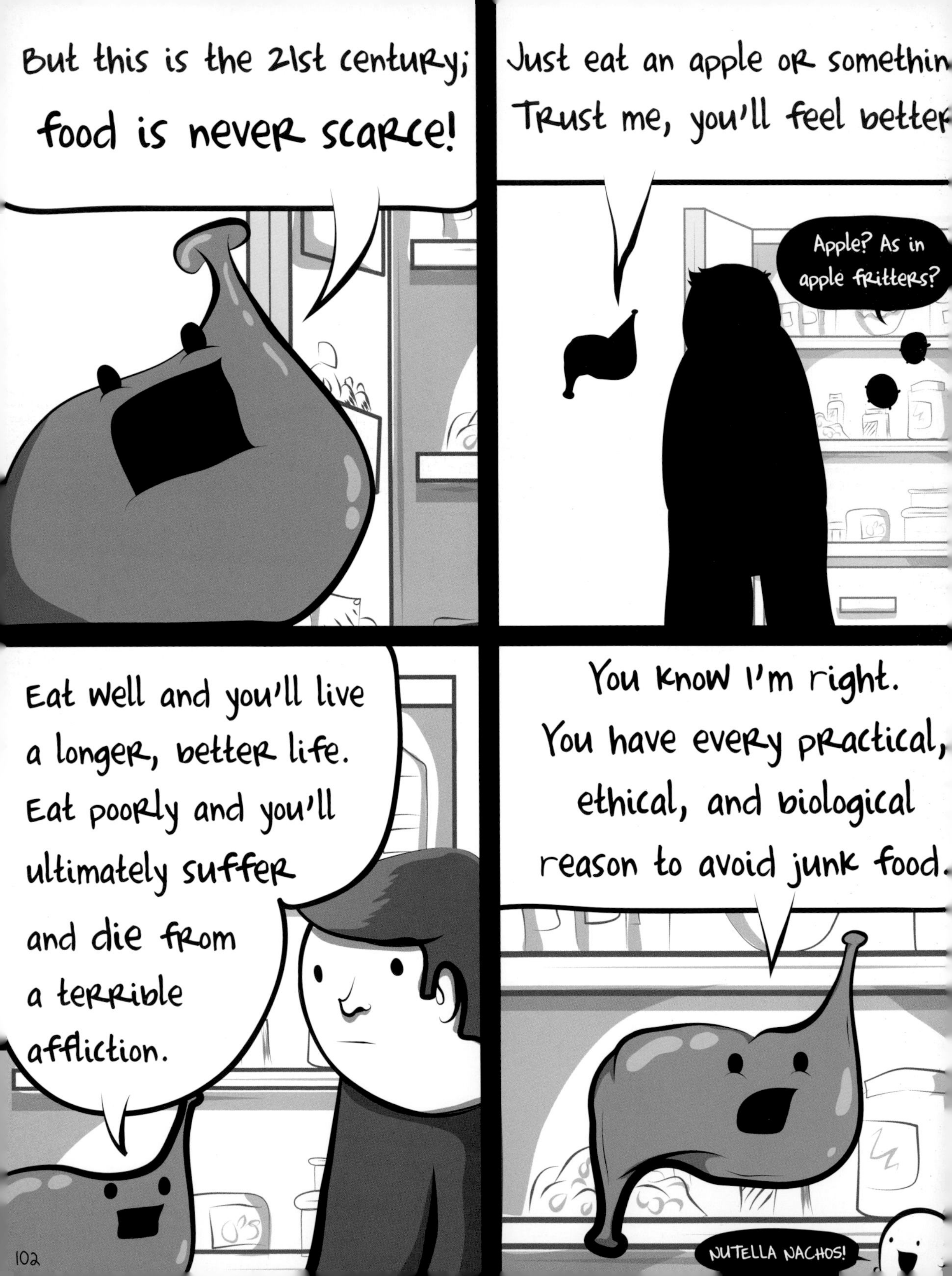
But this is the 21st century; food is never scarce!
Just eat an apple or somethin
Trust me, you'll feel better
Apple? As in apple fritters?
Eat well and you'll live a longer, better life. Eat poorly and you'll ultimately suffer and die from a terrible affliction.
You know I'm right. You have every practical, ethical, and biological reason to avoid junk food.
NUTELLA NACHOS!

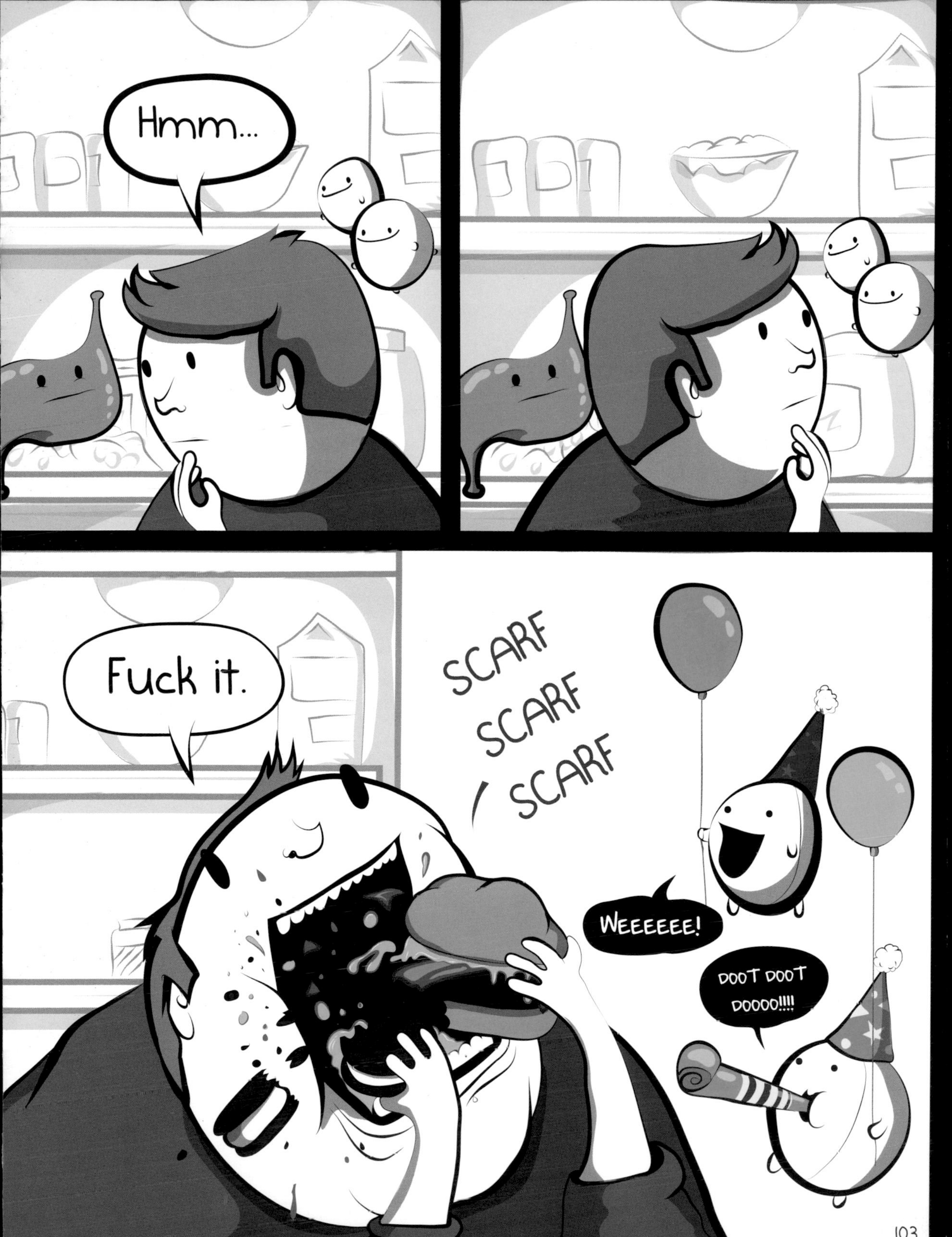
Hmm...
Fuck it.
SCARF
SCARF
SCARF
WEEEEEE!
DOOT DOOT
DOOOO!!!!

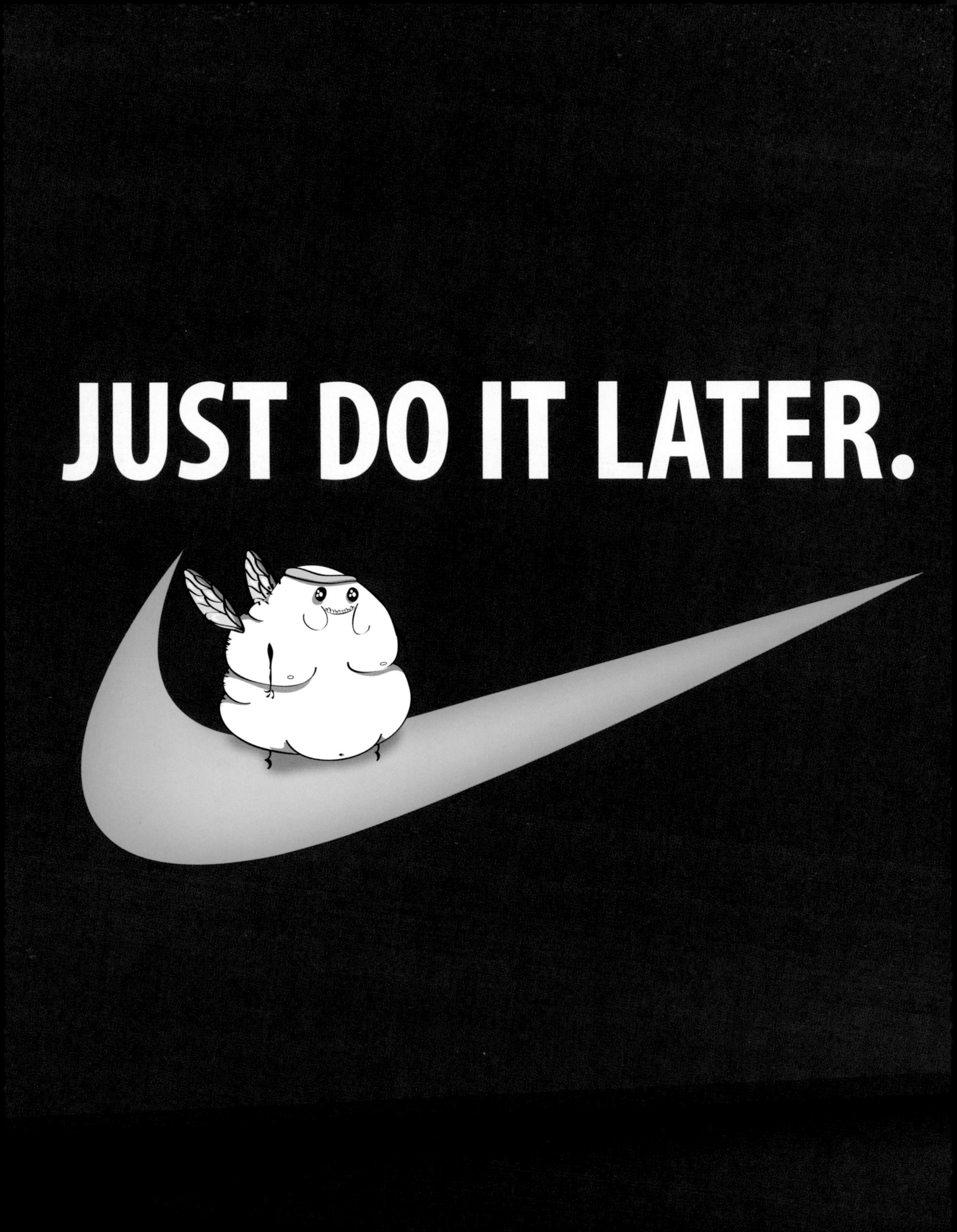
JUST DO IT LATER.

THERE'S NO RUSH.
HAVE A SNACK INSTEAD.
MAYBE A NAP, TOO.
SERIOUSLY, JUST TAKE IT EASY.
TAKE A LOAD OFF, BUDDY.
YOU EARNED IT.
EAT THE WHOLE CAKE.
EAT THE WHOLE GODDAMNED THING.

Things that make me run fast.

1. ~~Seeing an inspirational sign.~~ NOPE.

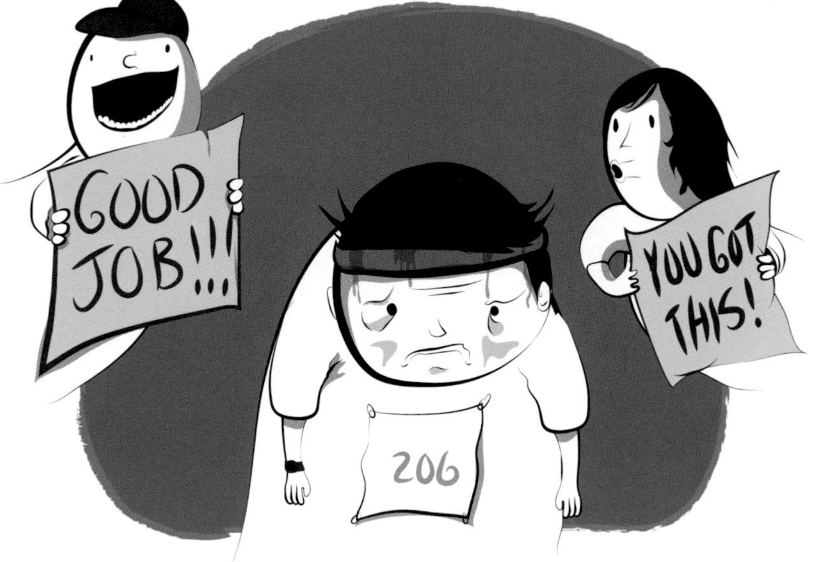
GOOD JOB!!!
YOU GOT THIS!
206

2. ~~Being told that if I sped up just a bit, I might set a new personal record~~. NOPE AGAIN.

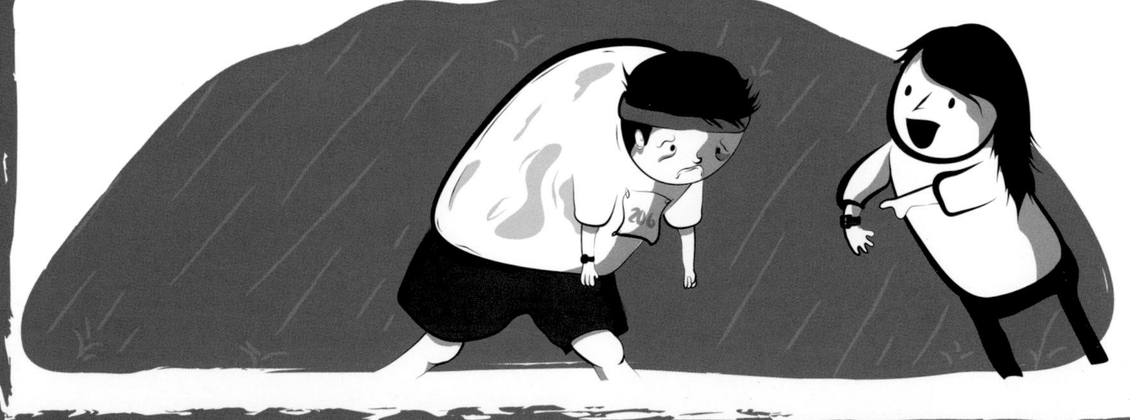
206

3. ~~Being near the finish line.~~ STILL NOPE.

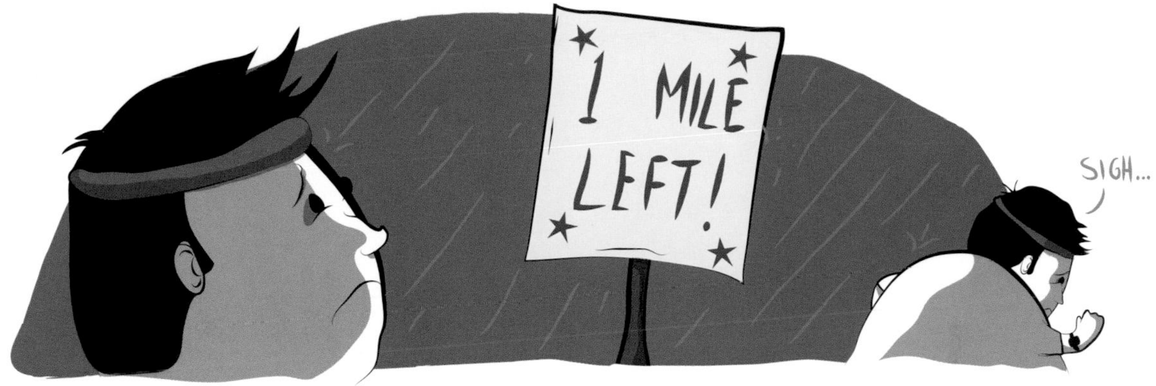
I MILE
LEFT!
SIGH...

4. Being passed by that one dude in the socks.

YUP.

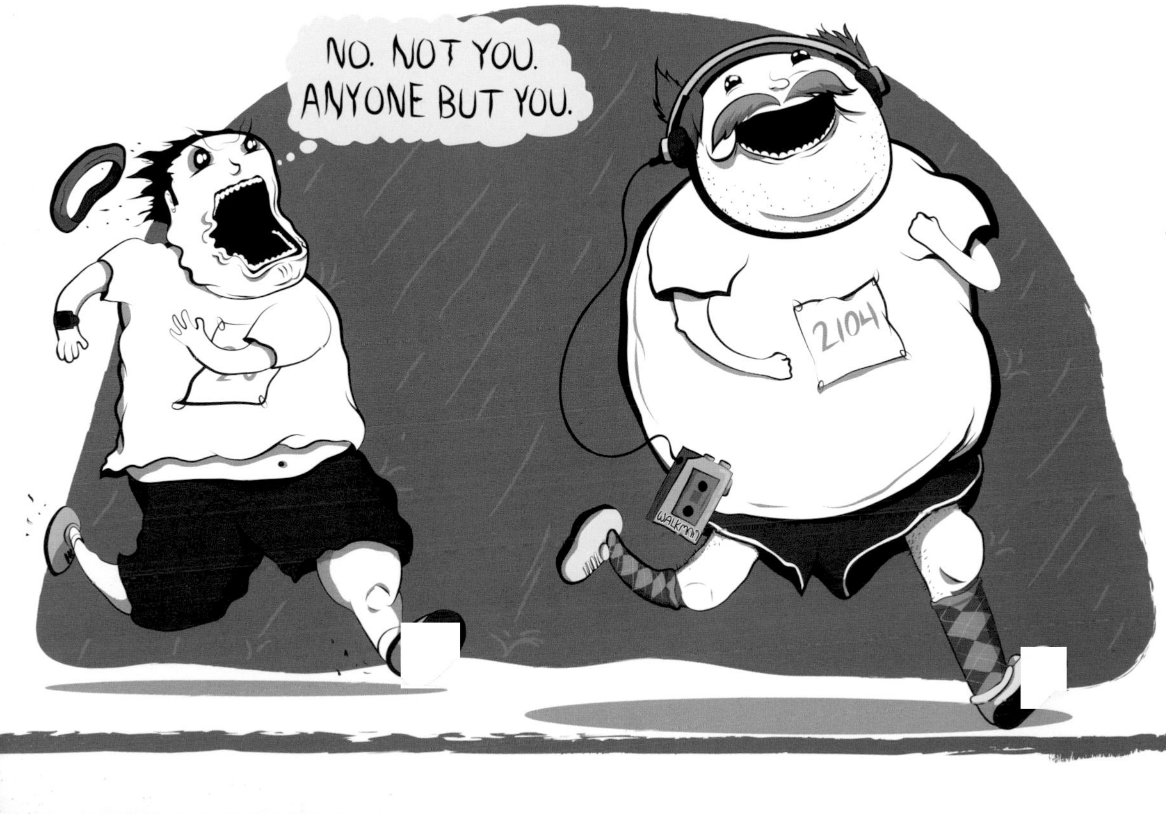
NO. NOT YOU.
ANYONE BUT YOU.
2104
WALKMAN

A lazy cartoonist's guide to becoming a runner

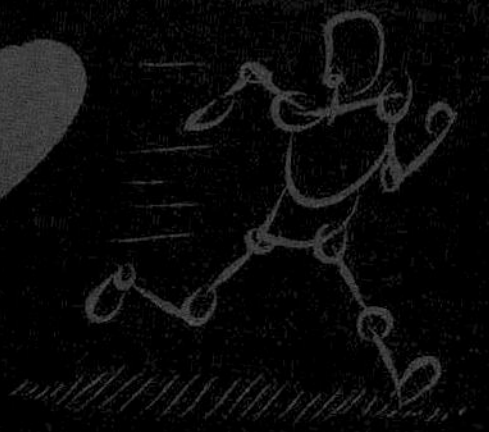

Many years ago, I found myself working a job where I was spending seventy hour weeks in front of a computer. Morning, noon, and night I was firmly planted on my butt, absorbed in a realm of slouching, snacking, clicking, and typing. After several years of this, I noticed that my body had begun to take on the shape of an overweight tyrannosaur.

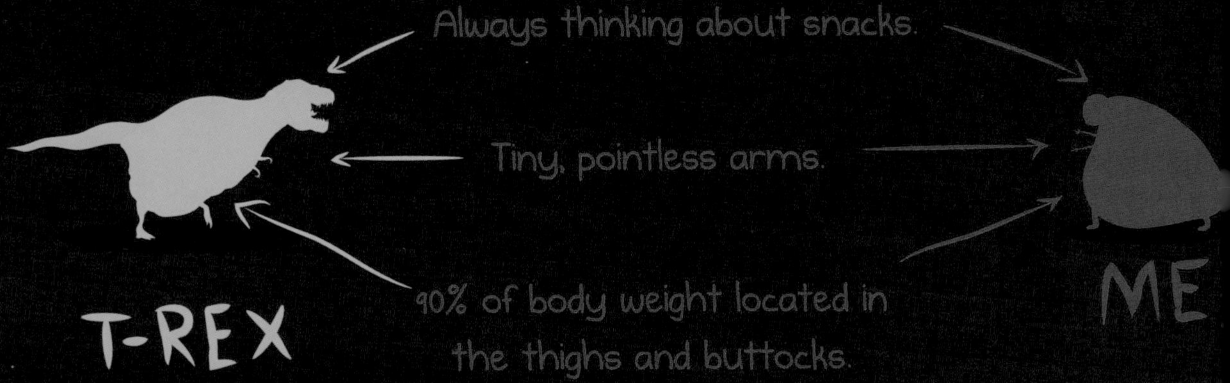

Always thinking about snacks.
Tiny, pointless arms.
90% of body weight located in the thighs and buttocks.
T-REX
ME

At first, this was okay.
I didn't mind a growing resemblance
to my Cretaceous doppelgänger.

What began to bother me, however, was that I was spending my entire life staring into glowing plastic boxes all day.

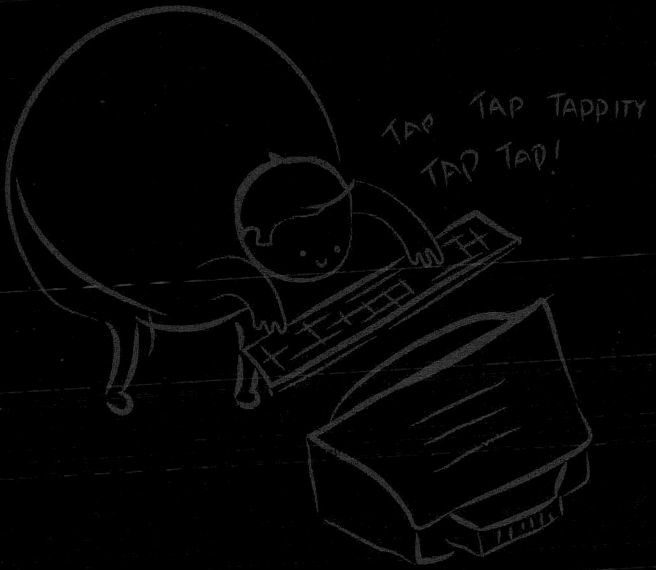
TAP TAP TAPPITY
TAP TAP!

So, on one chilly spring evening of no particular consequence, I went for a run.

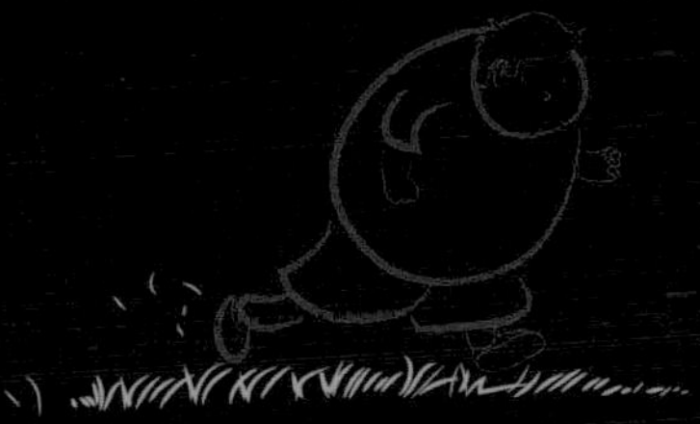

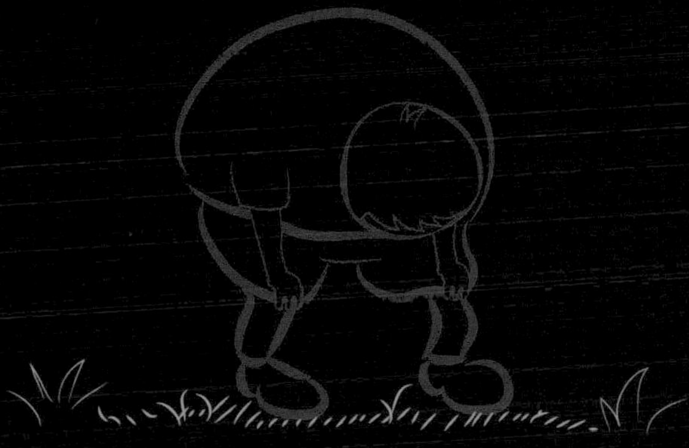

I didn't get far. I hadn't exercised in years so I could only go for a few minutes.

The next day I ran again,

and I was able to make it a little bit farther.
The day after that I ran almost a mile,
and the day after that I ran OVER a mile.

This pattern continued, day after day, week after week,
and within a few months I'd lost nearly 40 pounds,
dropped three pant sizes, and outpaced one
very cumbersome dinosaur.

I did not become a runner to lose weight,
I did it to escape my computer.

I started running to *feel* better, not to *look* better,
and I have created this guide with that philosophy in mind.

This is not a step by step guide to drastically losing weight or
getting six pack abs or completing a marathon.
It's a collection of things I did to make running *stick*.

Think of it as a deranged, rambling meditation from one
former T-rex to another.

Some of it isn't pretty,
and some of it isn't for everyone,
but it's what worked for me.

1. Shut up and run.

You'll never run out of reasons to take it easy. Your brain, body, and circumstances are all working around the clock to convince you to sit comfortably on those marvelous bum-cushions of yours.

"The weather sucks today."

"I'm slightly sleepier than usual."

"I worked out really hard the other day, so today I'll just take it easy."

"My favorite running socks are super stinky."

"I'll start exercising on Monday. Mondays are better for forming new habi

"That squirrel in the front yard is really mean and scary."

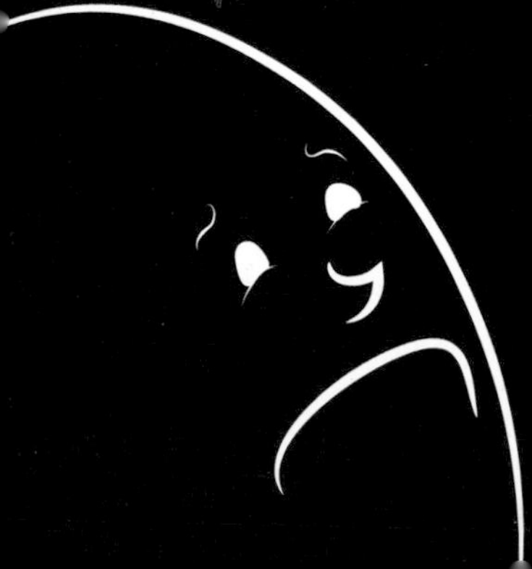

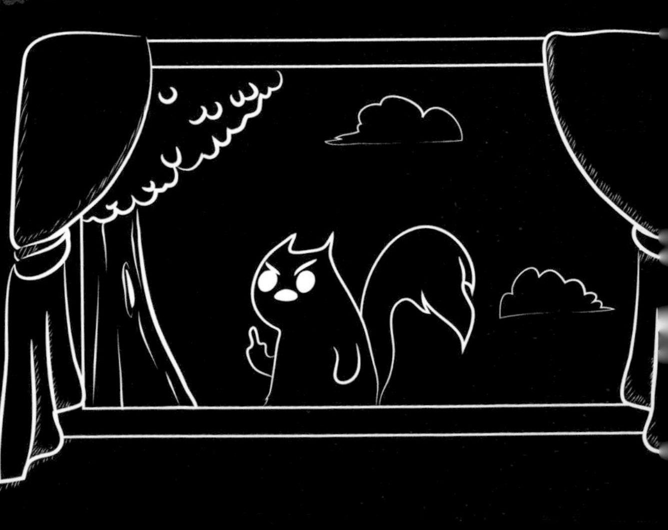

If you find yourself debating whether or not
you should go exercise,
it means you have the time and the means,
you're simply talking yourself out of
doing something difficult.

DO NOT participate in this debate.
Do not engage that apathetic little beast.
Don't even look him in the eye.
It's an argument you're going to lose.

Just put your shoes on and GET OUTSIDE.

Pretend your butt cheeks are a pair of cruise missiles.

Cruise missiles are meant to be launched.

They were destined to CRUISE, SOAR, AND OBLITERATE.

And that's exactly what you're doing.
This is outright war against a bottomless supply of excuses.
It is a blitzkrieg of the buttocks.

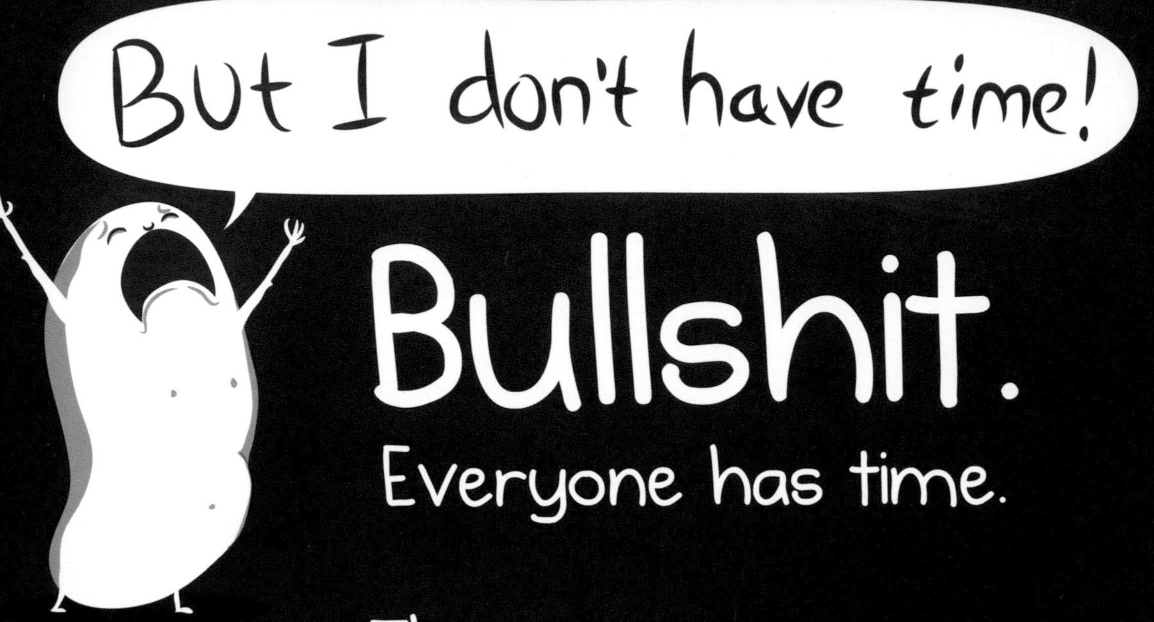
But I don't have time!

Bullshit.

Everyone has time.

There are

one thousand
four hundred
and forty minutes

in a day.

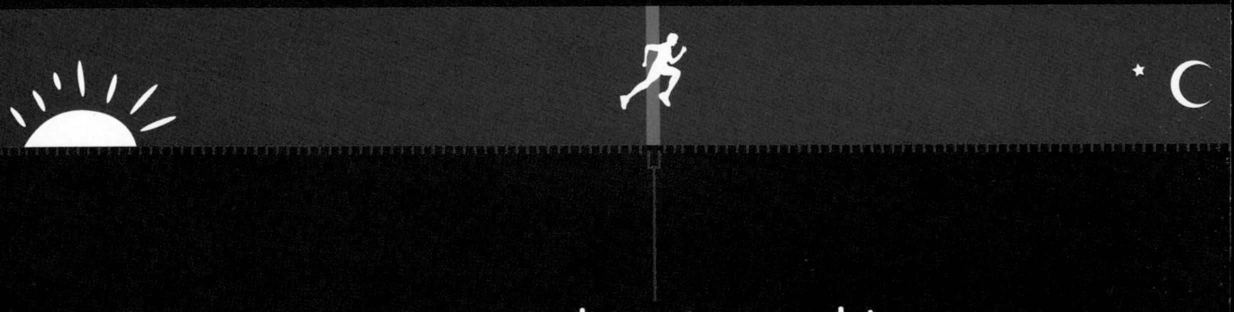

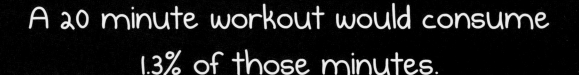

A 20 minute workout would consume 1.3% of those minutes.

If you're feeling terrible or melancholy or gluttonous
and you're not willing to devote one percent
of your day to being physically active,
then you don't DESERVE to feel better.

You haven't earned it.

You must swallow that teaspoon of sweaty discomfort
in order to receive your gallon of unbridled happy juice.

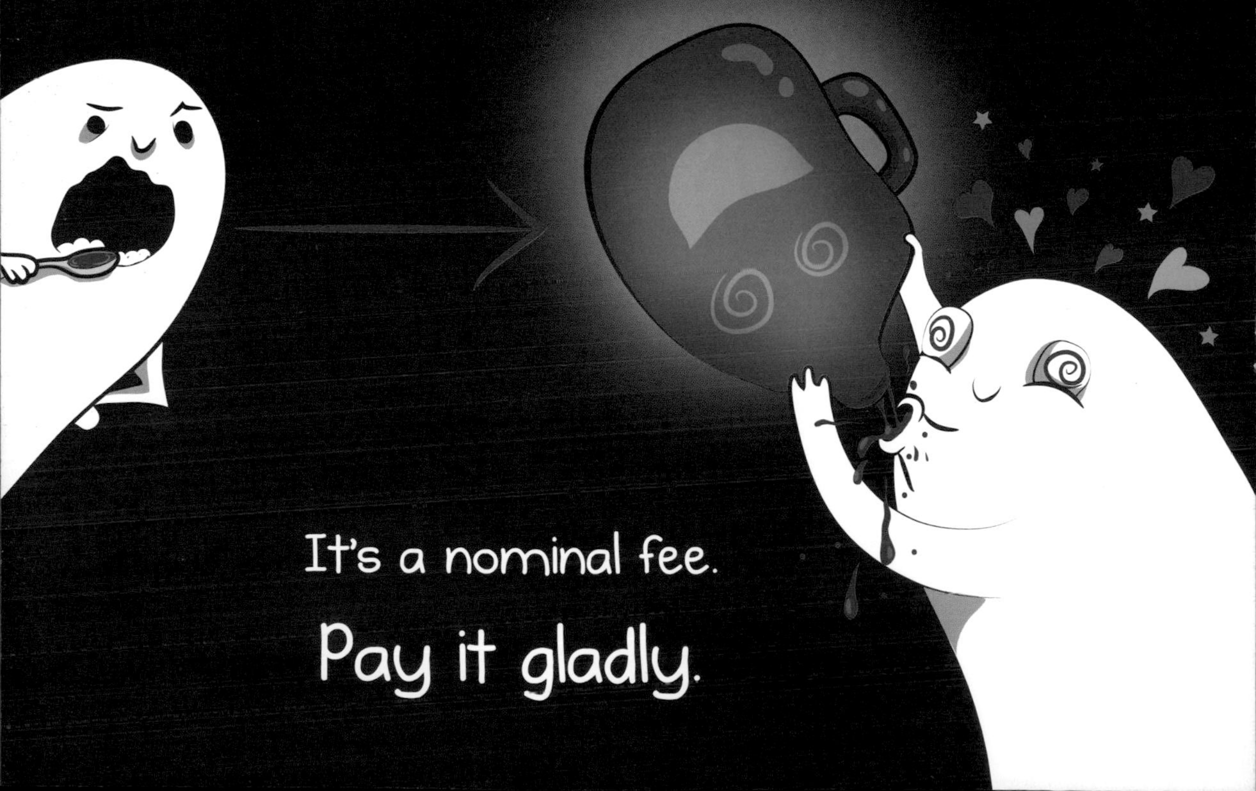

It's a nominal fee.

Pay it gladly.

2. Don't try to change a bunch of habits at once.

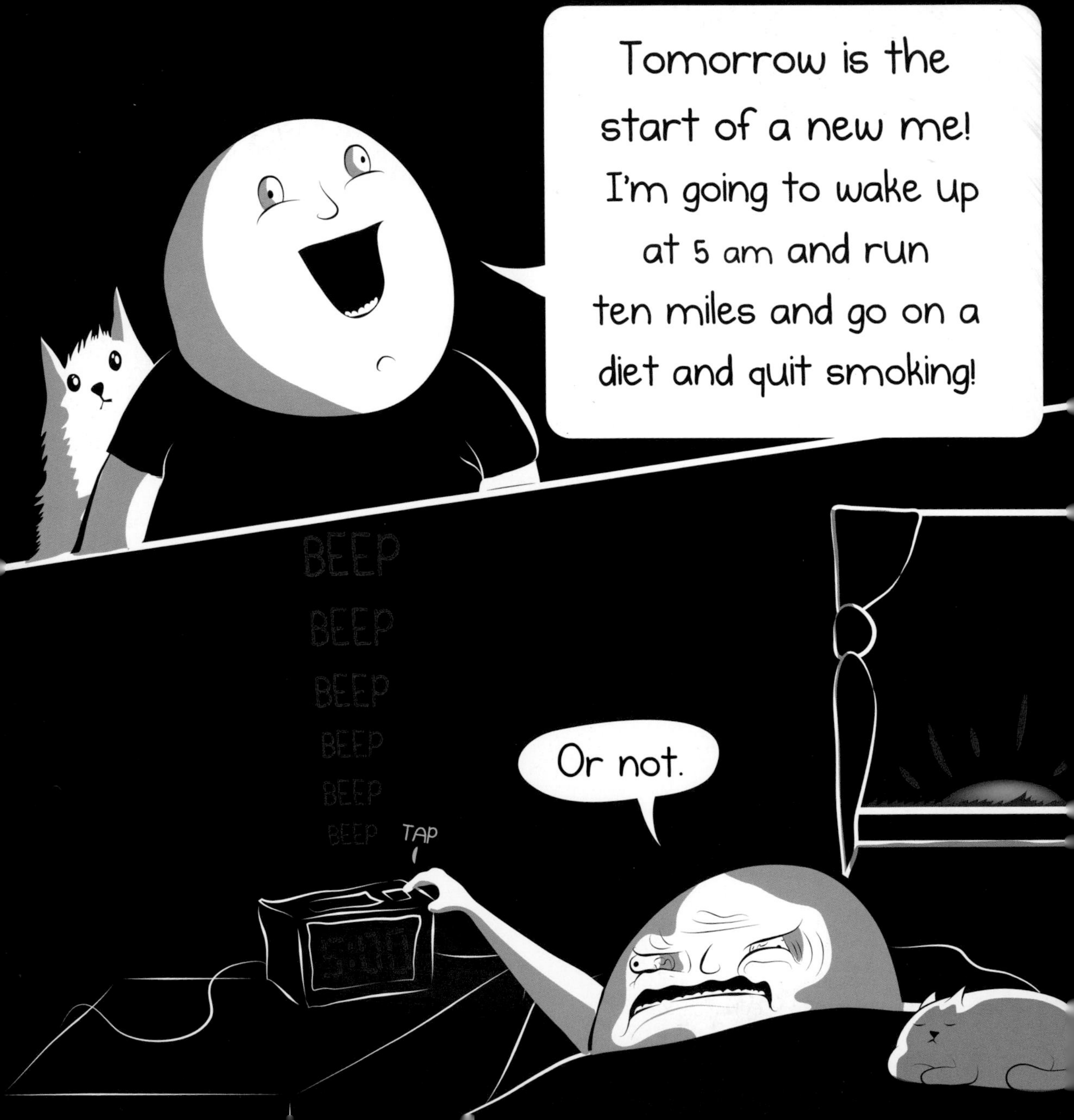

Giving up smoking is hard.
Waking up early is unnatural.
Dieting is frustrating.
Running hurts.

When you combine these goals into a single four-legged beast, all it takes is one of those legs to buckle and everything crashes down.

It is a brittle way of eliciting change.

Instead, craft a beast that sits firmly upon one leg.

Change one habit at a time.

Otherwise you're just setting yourself up for failure.

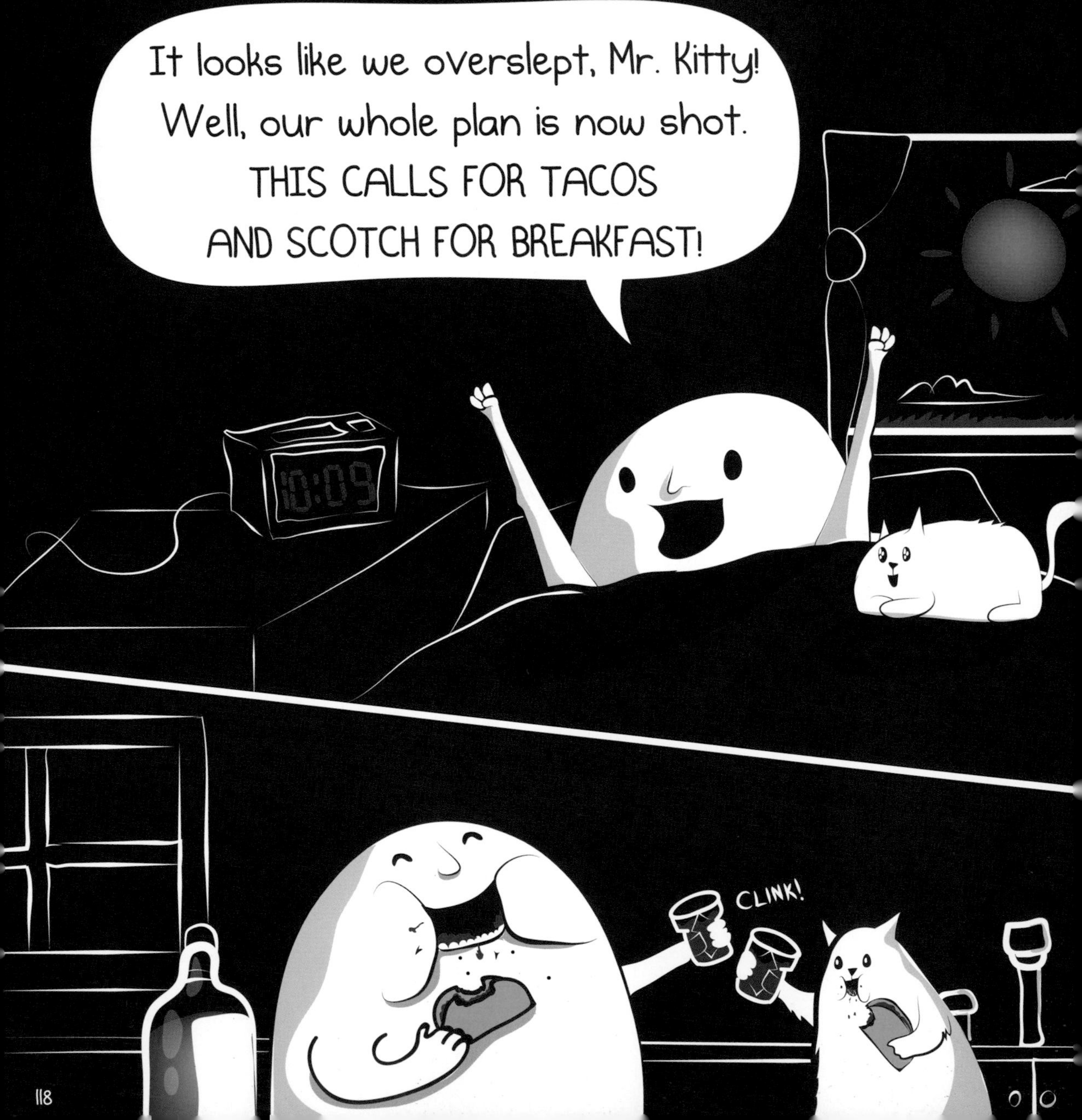
It looks like we overslept, Mr. Kitty! Well, our whole plan is now shot. THIS CALLS FOR TACOS AND SCOTCH FOR BREAKFAST!
10:09
CLINK!

ALSO,

've been running long distances for nearly ten years now,
and even *I* don't wake up at 5 am to exercise.
I run when I *need* to, not when I'm *supposed* to,
and I don't typically *need* to do anything at 5 am except
dream, fart, and sleep.

Many endurance athletes insist on waking up
super early to train. I am not one of those athletes.
I'm a runner, not a fucking werewolf.

There is nothing good about 5 am.
In the Bible it clearly states that 5 am is the hour
in which Satan gets a big angry demon boner.

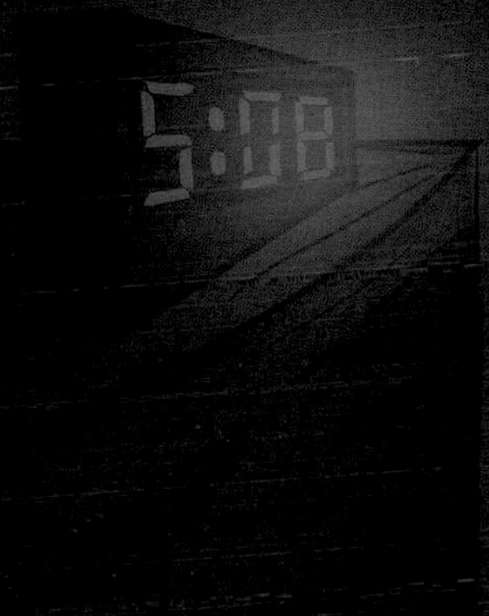

5:08

It is a wretched time.
Stay away from it.

3. Remember: running sucks in the beginning.

If you've never run farther than a mile in your entire life, I'm willing to bet you hate running—and understandably so, you've only experienced the crappy part.

You've never peeked beyond those first few minutes of torment. You don't know the raging tiki party of bliss that lies beyond.

10 minutes
My lungs are burning. I hate running.
20 minutes
My legs ache right now. I hate running.
30+ minutes
My nards are chafing.
RUNNING IS
SUPER

If you tell a non-runner that you ran a full marathon, all 26.2 miles of it, they'll say something like this:

26.2 miles?! That's 26.2 times harder than running ONE mile! That's incredible! You're incredible!

I'm incredible.

But, as most runners know, this isn't how it works.
It's easier than that. I'm not saying it's *easy*,
I'm simply saying that it's not 26.2 times *harder*.

Running sucks in the beginning. There are burning lungs and tired muscles and heaps of misery and frustration.
But it doesn't stay that way.

It's a front-loaded chore.

Starting out, your body is going to fight you. It's got a vested interest in keeping you fat, comfortable, and warm—and it's going to protect that interest. Whether it's the first few minutes of a run or the first few weeks of training, that hairy meat tricycle of yours is going to give you plenty of reasons to go sit down.

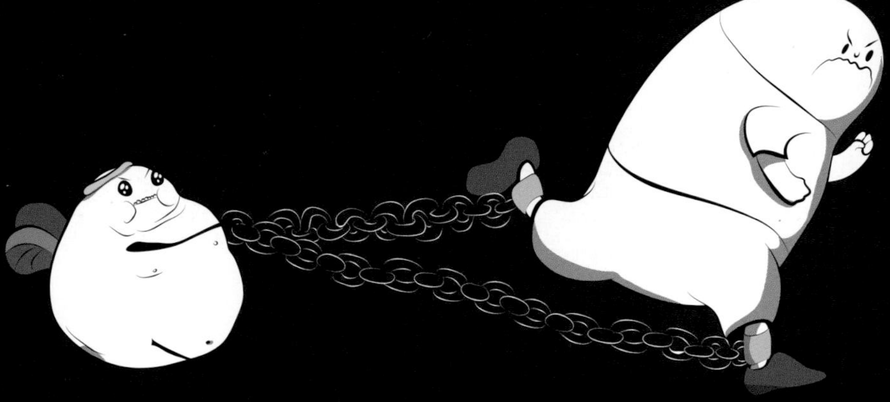

You just have to keep going.
You have to win that argument against your body.

After that you're free.

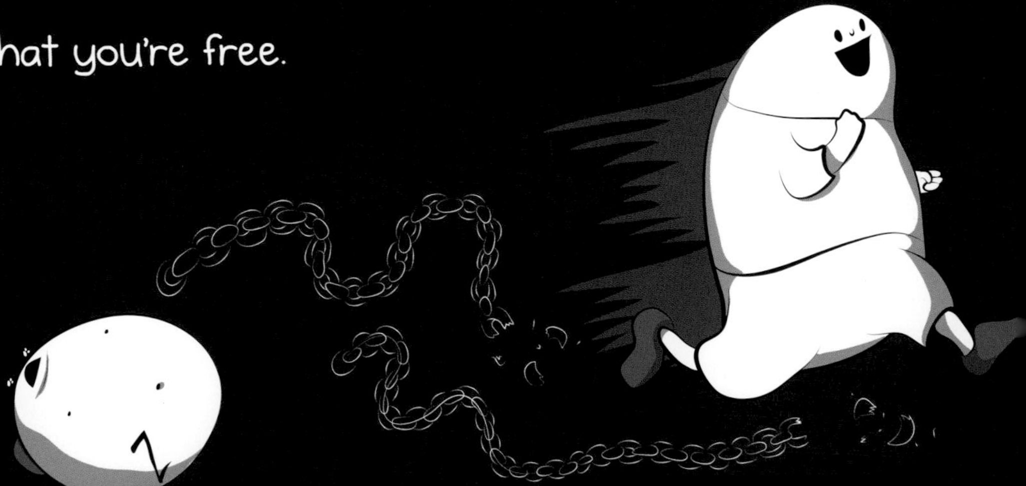

If you find yourself hating running

and quitting early,

just keep at it.

Running takes time to become enjoyable.

It's not a surgical strike; it's a war of attrition.

And any war that ends with a tiki party is a war worth fighting.

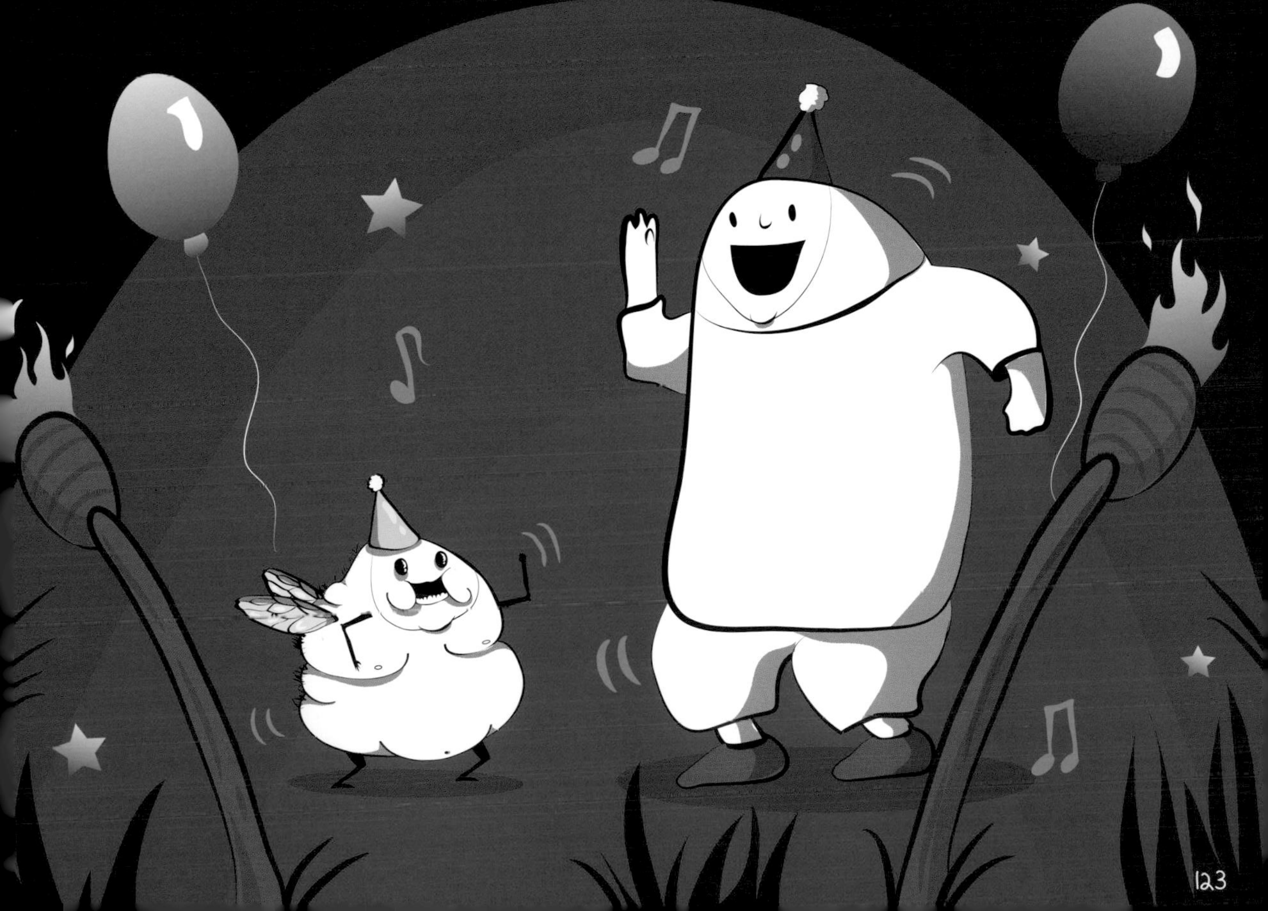

4. Run outside.

If you want to hate running,
I highly recommend using a treadmill.

It's a fun little device. It enables you to sweat in place while being taunted by a glowing panel of decrementing integers which maddeningly remind you of how much longer things are going to suck.

It is like being taunted by a cyborg.
A cyborg never tires.
A cyborg does not know fatigue.
A cyborg knows only
ones and zeros.

Cyborgs are dicks.

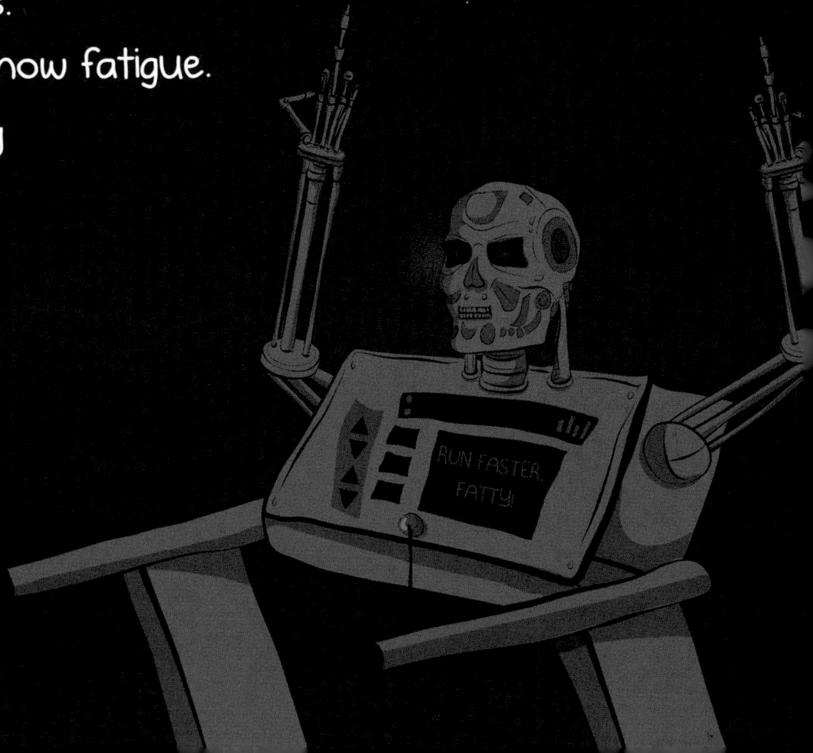
RUN FASTER, FATTY!

If possible, find a loop.

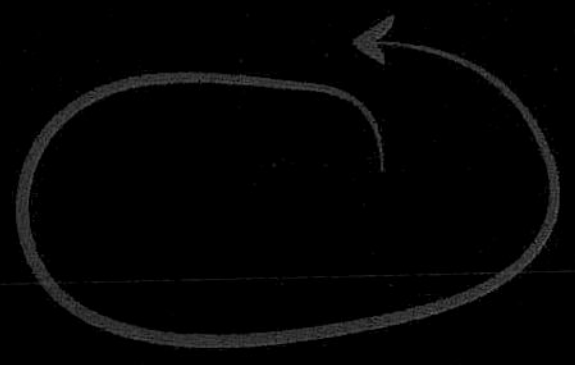

Run in a big, looped course outside,

deally just beyond the perimeter of your comfort zone.

A treadmill enables you to push a bright red quit button
at any time, but when you run a circular course,
you're *forced* to make the return trip home.

I've noticed that when I run on a
treadmill or an out-and-back course,
I almost always quit early.

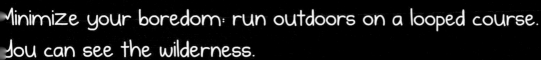

FUCK IT.

Minimize your boredom: run outdoors on a looped course.
You can see the wilderness.
You can see the cityscape.
Maybe you'll see a ain ow.
Maybe you'll see a caribou taking a dump.

Whatever you see,
you'll only have to see it once.

You are mitigating monotony.

Sure, on a treadmill you can distract yourself with music or TV, but I run to get out of the house and *feel* better, not to burn calories while catching up on bad TV.

Running is an accessible sport: all you need is a pair of shoes and a wide, open space. Embrace that accessibility and run outside.

{ I treat a run as if it were a hike. When I go hiking, I have a rough idea of where I'm going and generally how long it's going to take, but I don't dwell on pace, calories, or mileage. I'm not robotically counting my steps and quitting the hike as soon as I hit an arbitrary number. }

I understand that some people simply *can't* run outside.
Certain neighborhoods can be dangerous after dark.
There are muggers and quicksand and vampire bats and whatnot.

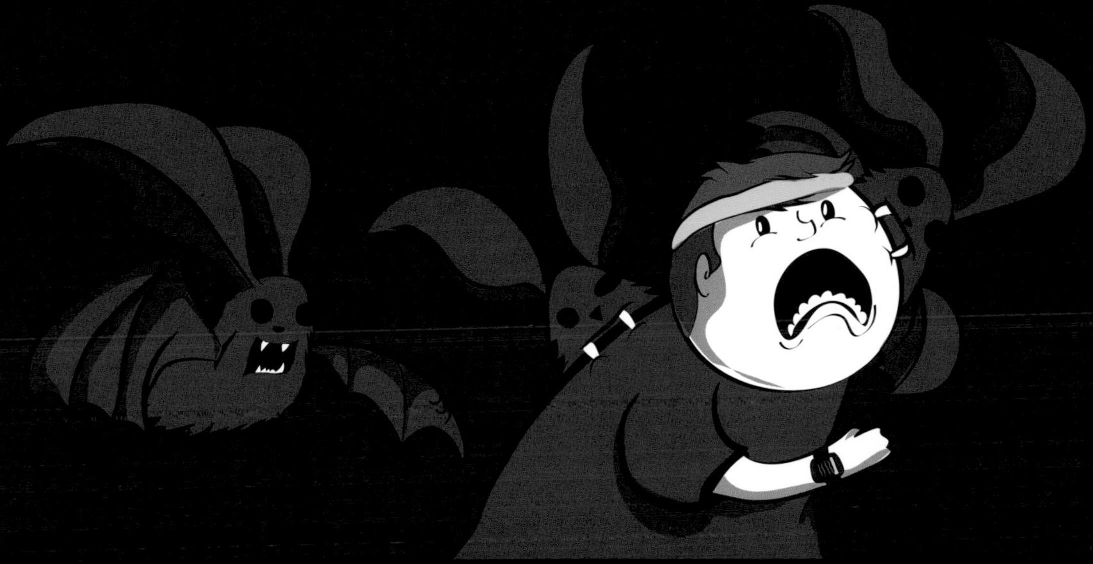

But, if a choice exists between a treadmill and the outdoors, choose the outdoors.

Choose bats, not cyborgs.

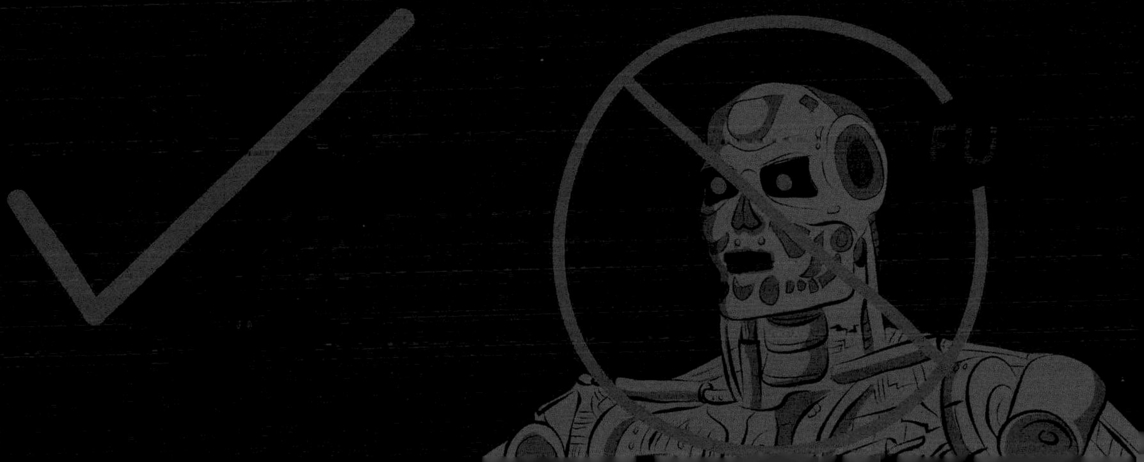

5. Sign up for an event.

Distance runners are manic beasts.

We often train alone, quietly shuffling along the pavement for hours on end—our only companion being a bottomless well of sweat, pain, and introspection. Even social runners—those who run in a group, often wind up drifting out of the pack and plodding along quietly at their own pace.

To a bystander, we may appear sullen or lonely,

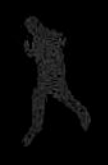

and maybe we are.

But on race day, that all changes.

A marathon is the collective release of thousands of hours of solitary tedium taking the form of a massive crowd of strangers all choosing to hurt themselves in exactly the same way.

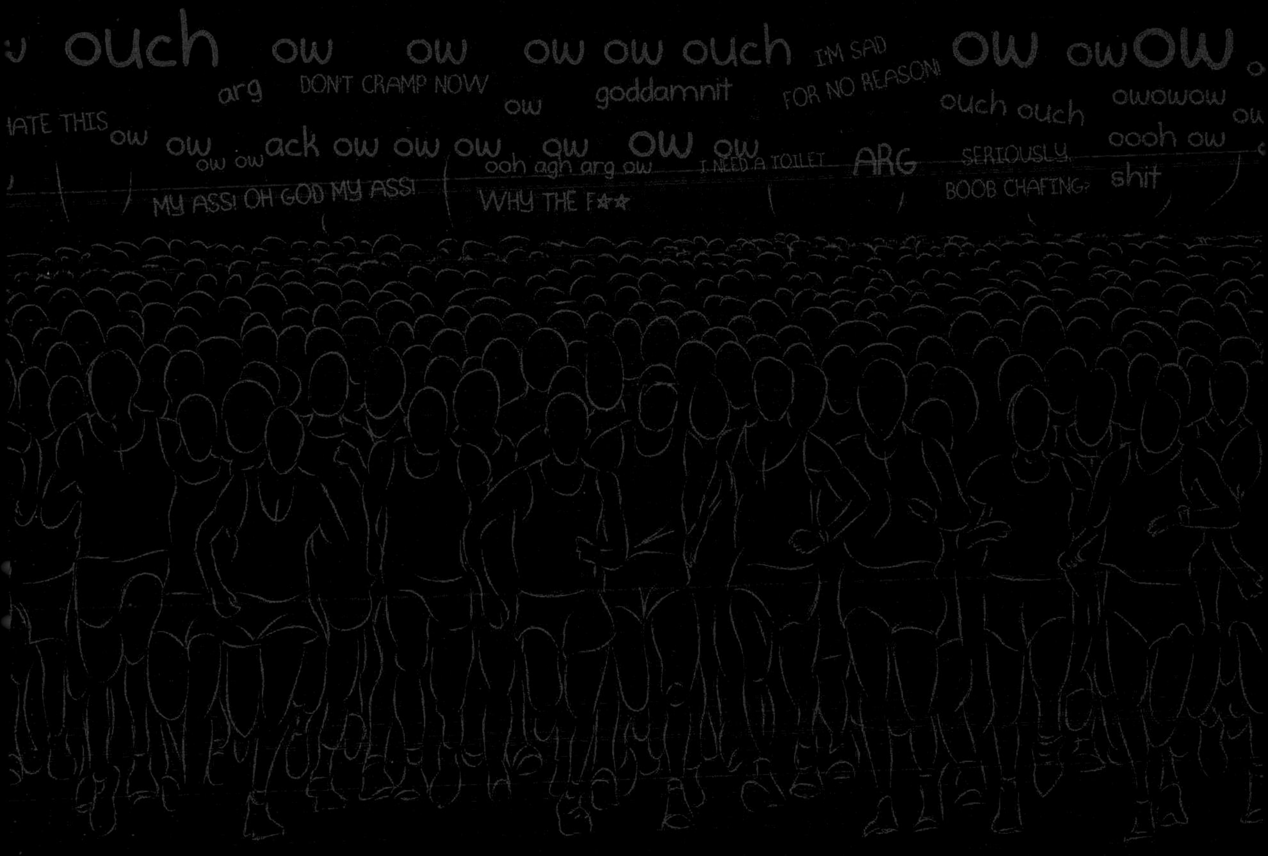

ouch
ow
ow
ow ow ouch
I'M SAD FOR NO REASON!
OW owOW
arg
DON'T CRAMP NOW
ow
goddamnit
ouch ouch
owowow
HATE THIS
ow
ow
ow ow
ack ow ow ow
ow
OW
ow
ooh ow
ooh agh arg ow
I NEED A TOILET
ARG
SERIOUSLY, BOOB CHAFING?
shit
MY ASS! OH GOD MY ASS!
WHY THE F★★

It's wonderful. Or awful.

It's both, really.

The entire spectrum of human emotion is at play during a marathon.

It's an experience that's hard to put into words.

The closest comparison I can think of is if ten thousand pregnant ladies all met in the street and started firing infants out of their hoo-haws in a massive game of amniotic paintball.

It would be a messy ordeal.

There would be sweat.
There would be tears.
There would be police cars and barricades.

But in the end, an army of countless baby-people would emerge, all feasting on orange slices and high-fiving one another for a job well done.

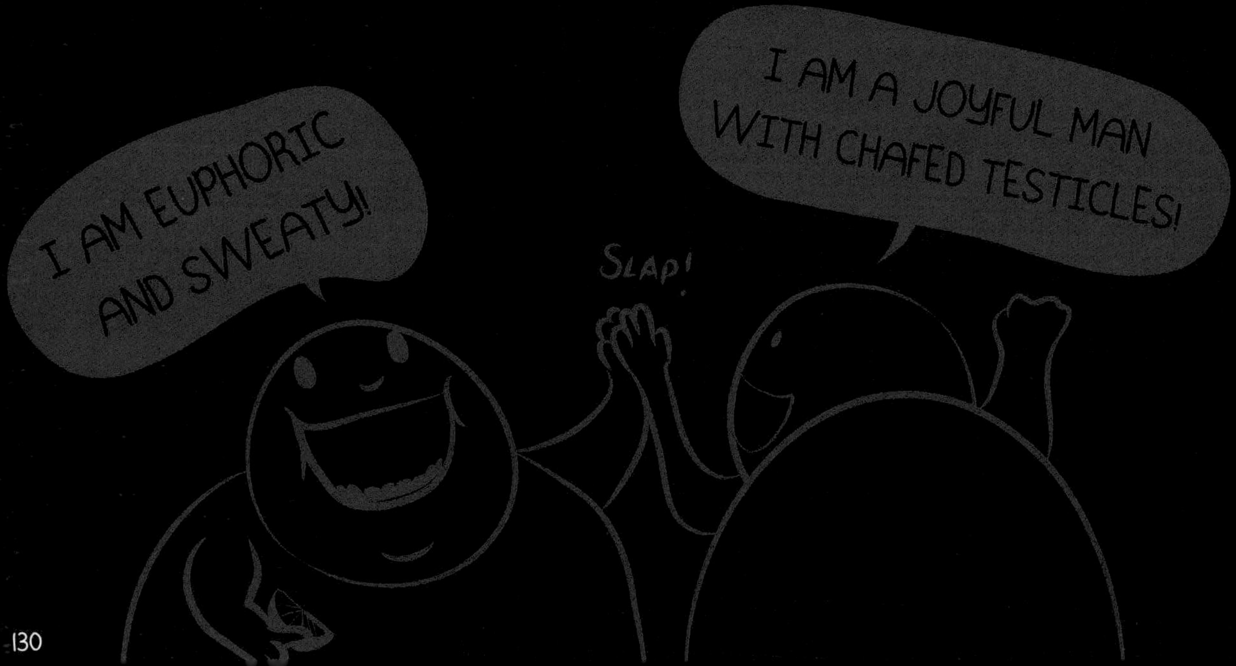
I AM EUPHORIC AND SWEATY!
SLAP!
I AM A JOYFUL MAN WITH CHAFED TESTICLES!

I'm not sure this analogy makes sense.

FORGET THE BABIES.

What I'm trying to say is this:

Running a race assigns a POINT to a sport that often feels very POINTLESS.

It's an exuberant payoff to months of tedium.

It's a way of crafting an end boss for a particularly cumbersome video game.

It's a fun, monstrous reason to keep putting one foot in front of the other.

So, do yourself a favor: go build a monster.

Sign up for a race.

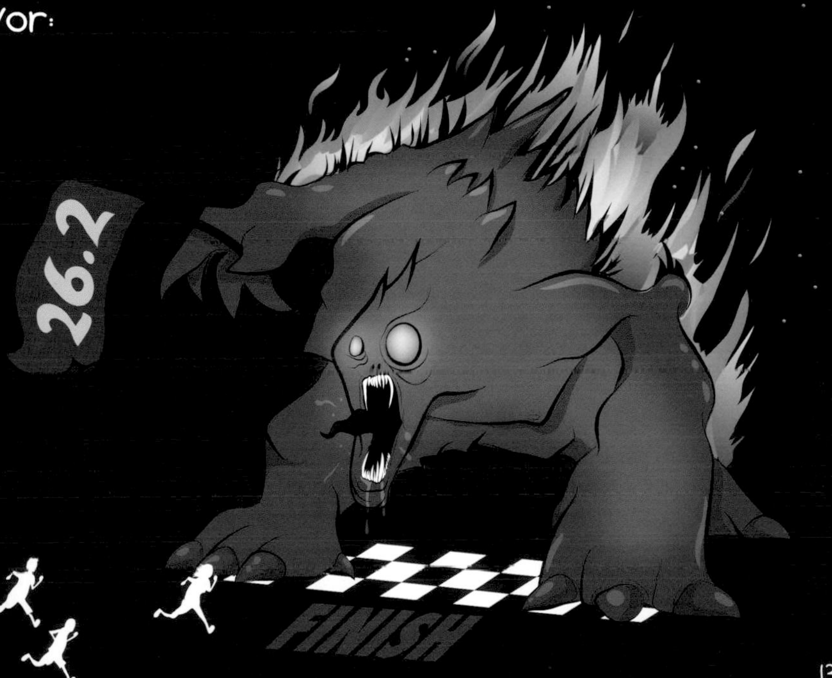
26.2
FINISH

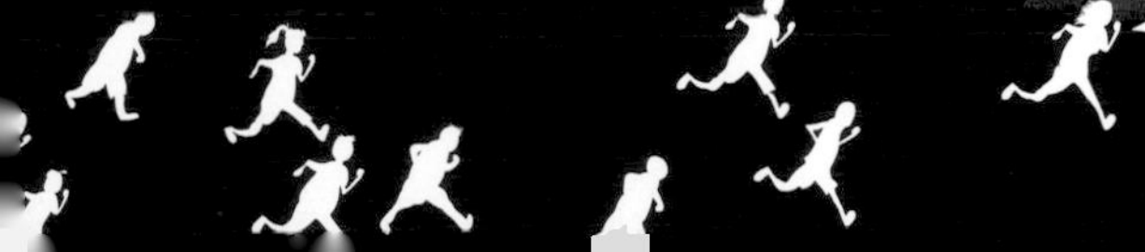

6. Don't think ahead.

I've spent most of my life living fifteen minutes in the future. If I'm at a restaurant enjoying a tasty beer, my mind is focused on the meal I just ordered. If I'm eating that meal, I'm thinking about dessert. If I'm eating dessert, I'm thinking about catching a movie after dinner.

I'm never *present*—I'm dwelling on the next *exciting-fun-treat* that's headed my way.

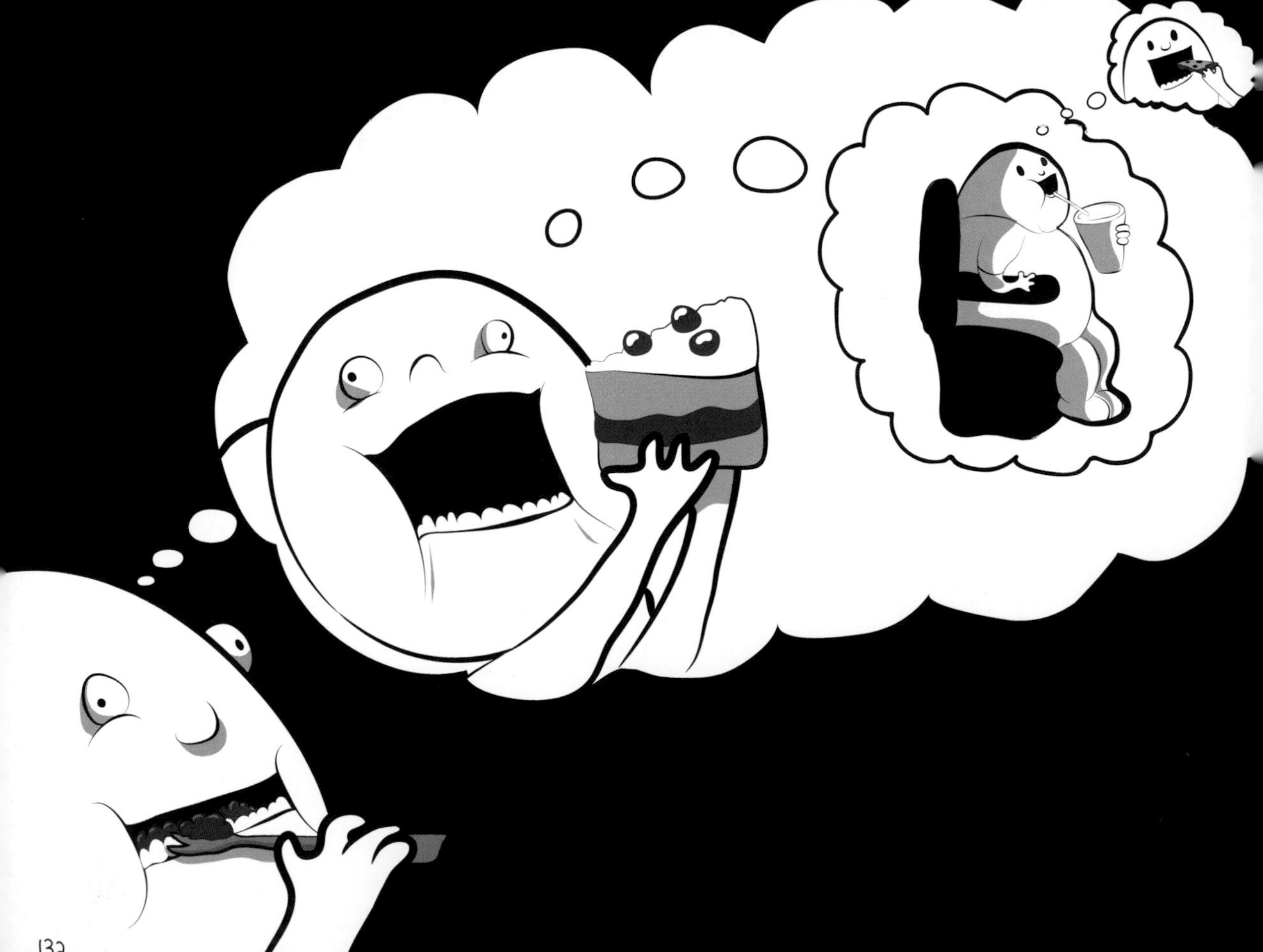

Running hurts.

Running will *always* hurt. You do get used to it, and the pain certainly diminishes, but there's always a certain degree of suffering.

I work very hard to *own* this suffering. Much like eating, I try to NOT live in the future. I don't dwell on my next reward and count the seconds until my next awesome-special-feel-good-surprise.

I possess my circumstances,
whether they're terrible, wonderful, or somewhere in between.

I'M TENTACLED :(

I'M NAKED ...
WHICH IS ILLEGAL!

I'M SUPER MAD BECAUSE
MY HEAD IS ON FIRE!

It's easy to be philosophical about this.
It's much harder to actually *do* it.

I've adopted a little mantra that sometimes helps:

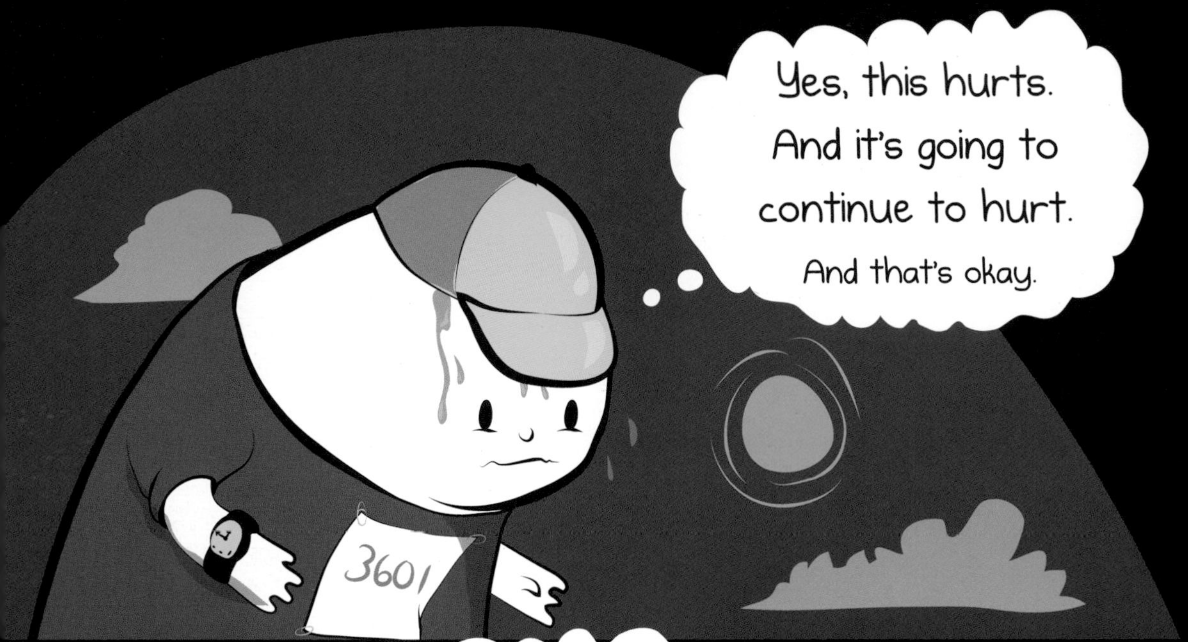
Yes, this hurts.
And it's going to
continue to hurt.
And that's okay.
3601

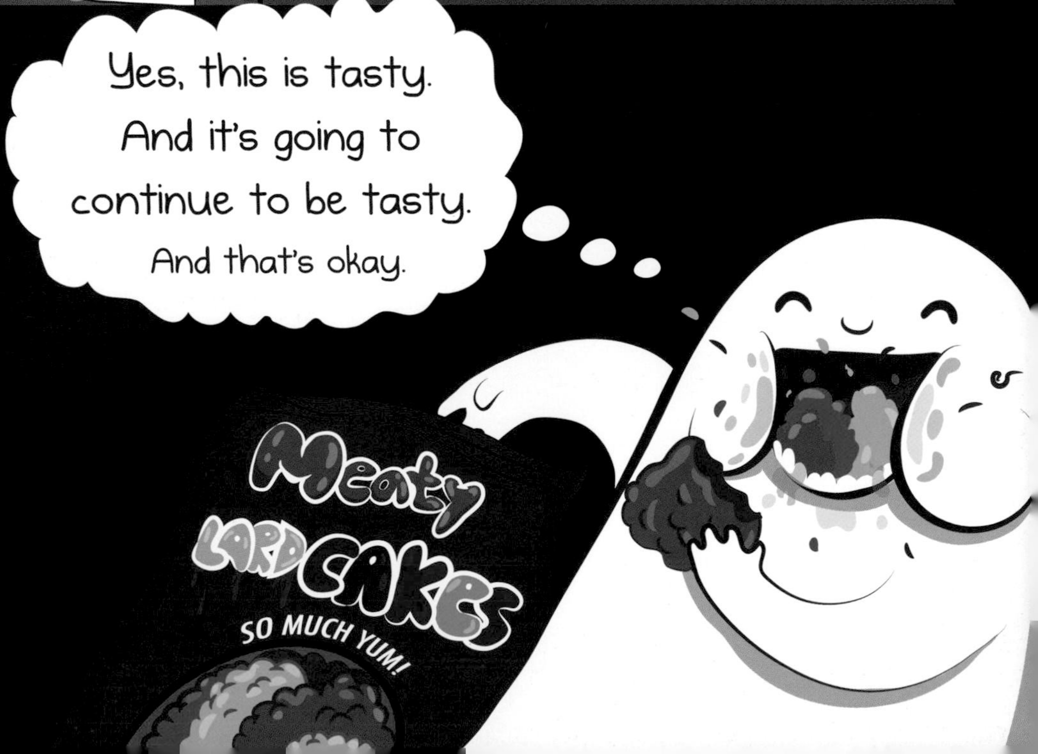
Yes, this is tasty.
And it's going to
continue to be tasty.
And that's okay.
Meaty
LARD CAKES
SO MUCH YUM!

Some people choose NOT to cope with the tedium and pain of running, and instead **distract** themselves by listening to music or chatting with other runners. This can help pass the time, but it also waters down the core of what it takes to be a distance runner.

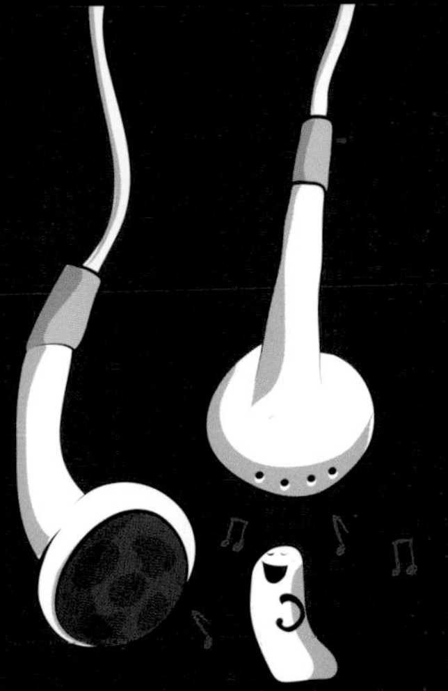

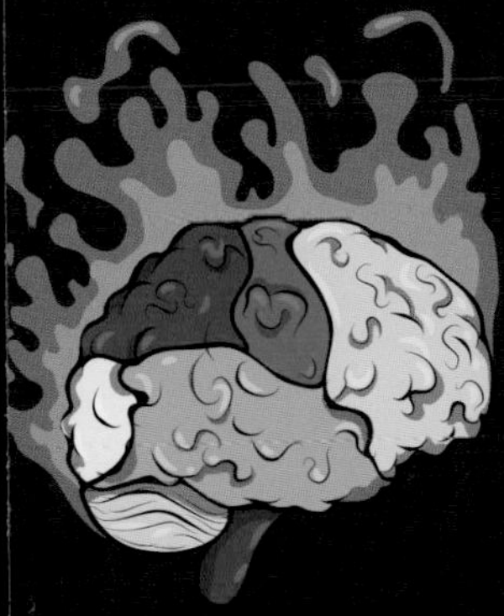

Running is a form of

practiced stoicism.

It means teaching your brain and body to be biomechanically comfortable in a state of disrepair.

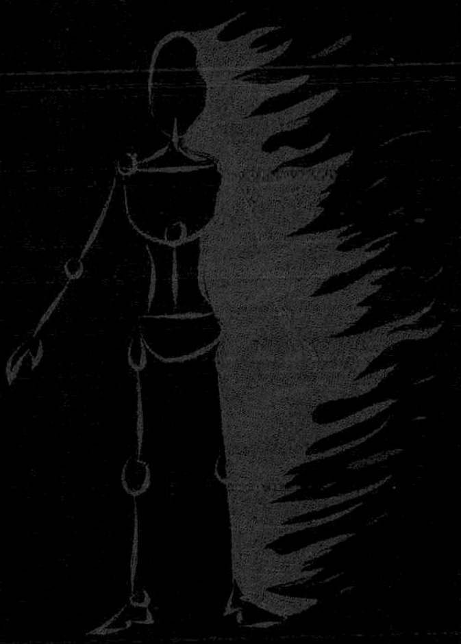

Distractions enable you to *put off* that discomfort — to procrastinate confronting an inexorable march of pain.

But pain and hardship are neither friend nor foe to a runner: **they're neighbors.**

They're familiar. A known quantity.

7. Become a drug addict.

I eat too much. I always have.

And I eat too fast. Food is not delicately placed into my face; it is *shoveled*. I eat snacks like I'm burying bodies in the dark: it's frantic and shameful and it frightens the neighbors.

And after 30+ years of overeating, I've taken a hard look at why I do this, and I've come to an understanding:

I overeat because food *tastes* good, but more importantly, I do it because it *feels* good.

It's a nine minute vacation.

It's a short dip into a shallow pool of chewing, tasting, and swallowing.

It's an escape for a greedy, fat, impulsive man-child who happens to be wearing grown-up clothes.

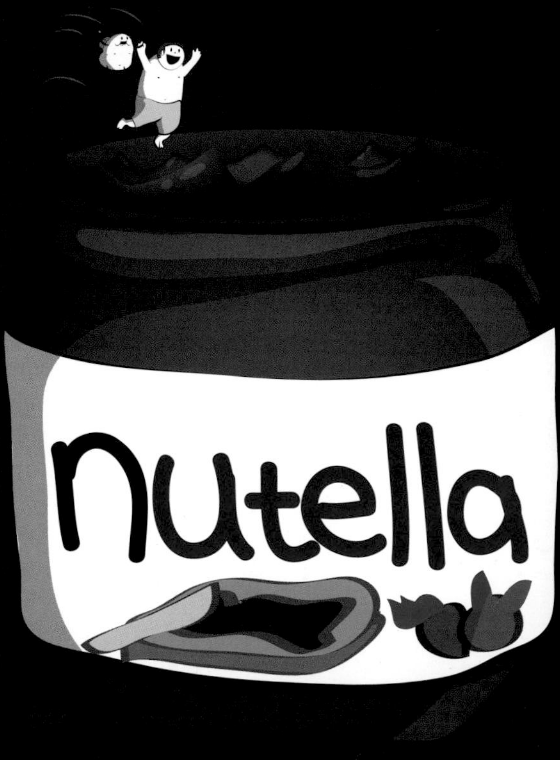
nutella

I often regard overeating as a drug addiction,

and I try to imagine what my life would be like if that addiction got the best of me. I picture the years wearing on, with earth's annual trip around the sun being marked by an increase in pant sizes and a decrease in self worth. I imagine my heart getting tighter and more flustered, until one sunny morning it shudders to a violent halt. I imagine myself wrenching forward, my face heaving into a pile of waffles. I imagine my last breath gurgling into a tepid pool of maple syrup.

I imagine all of these things, and I think:

I don't want to die face-first in a pile of waffles.

I want to die in an electrical storm.
I want to die wrestling a Kodiak bear.
I want to die in an EXPLOSION.

I want to die quietly at home,
hand in hand with somebody who loved me.

I just don't want to die by waffles. Anything but waffles.

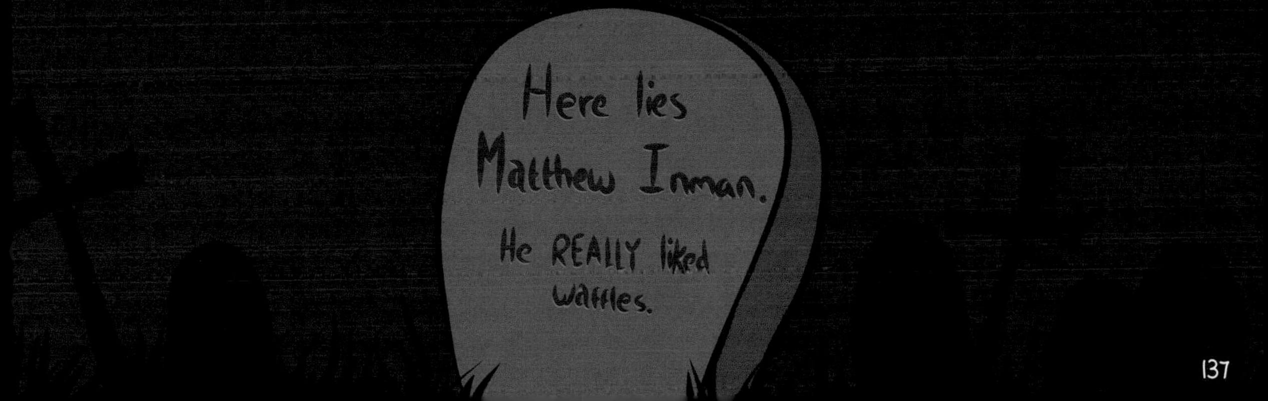
Here lies
Matthew Inman.
He REALLY liked
waffles.

And so,

motivated by fear,

I choose to be a different kind of drug addict:

I choose to be a runner.

And make no mistake: running *is* an addiction, both chemically and spiritually. There are euphoric highs, terrible lows, and the constant desire to "squeeze in a quick run" in order to feel whole.

But unlike other drug addictions, running is *socially acceptable*.

It's like being able to smoke crack every day, but instead of getting strung out and arrested you get bananas and compliments.

SMOKE CRACK AND ROLL
MARATHON

224

604

9571

And it's certainly more socially acceptable than dieting.

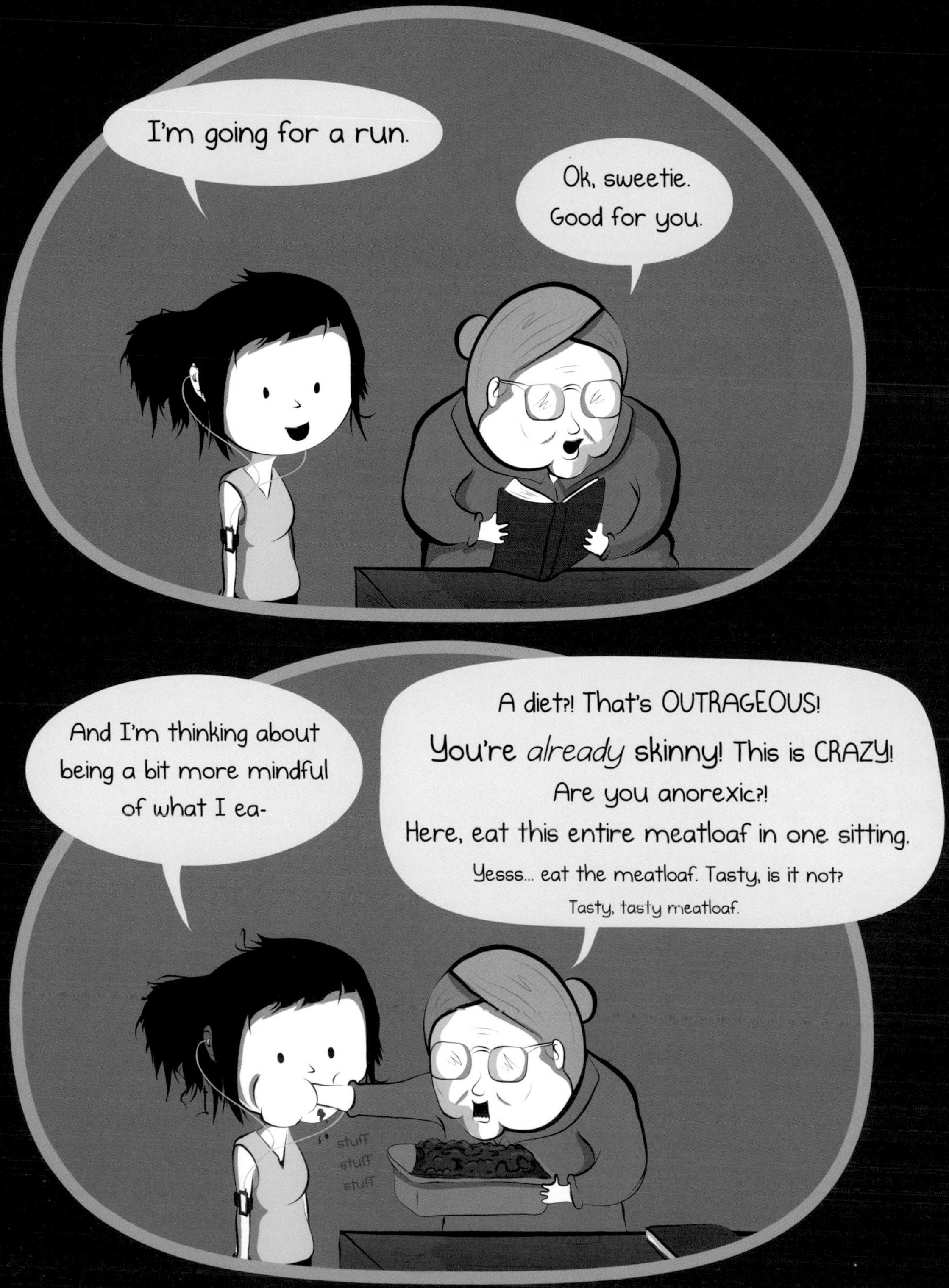
I'm going for a run.
Ok, sweetie. Good for you.
And I'm thinking about being a bit more mindful of what I ea-
A diet?! That's OUTRAGEOUS!
You're *already* skinny! This is CRAZY!
Are you anorexic?!
Here, eat this entire meatloaf in one sitting.
Yesss... eat the meatloaf. Tasty, is it not?
Tasty, tasty meatloaf.
stuff
stuff
stuff

Being a former fat kid was a motivator as well,

and I've often wondered it if was a blessing or a curse.
It turned me into an active, health-conscious adult, but I also
live with the daily fear that I'm on the verge of turning back
into a chubby little sad-monster.

Even now, decades later, I'm still convinced that I'm only a
few meals away from becoming Mr. Hyde with love handles.

It's a stupid, pointless worry,
but it's a worry that's here to stay.

So, to cope with that stupidity, I started running, and I eventually came to a point where something "broke" in my head. A *reversal* occurred, and it became more painful for me to remain sedentary than to be active.

I figured out that it hurt more to feel fat and depressed than to put on a pair of running shoes and log a few more miles in hell.

It's a nice place to be, I suppose,
this deranged little fitness nirvana, wherein the pain of depression outweighs the pain of physical torment.

Is this a healthy, responsible way to live?
Fuck it. Who cares.

It's better than the waffles.

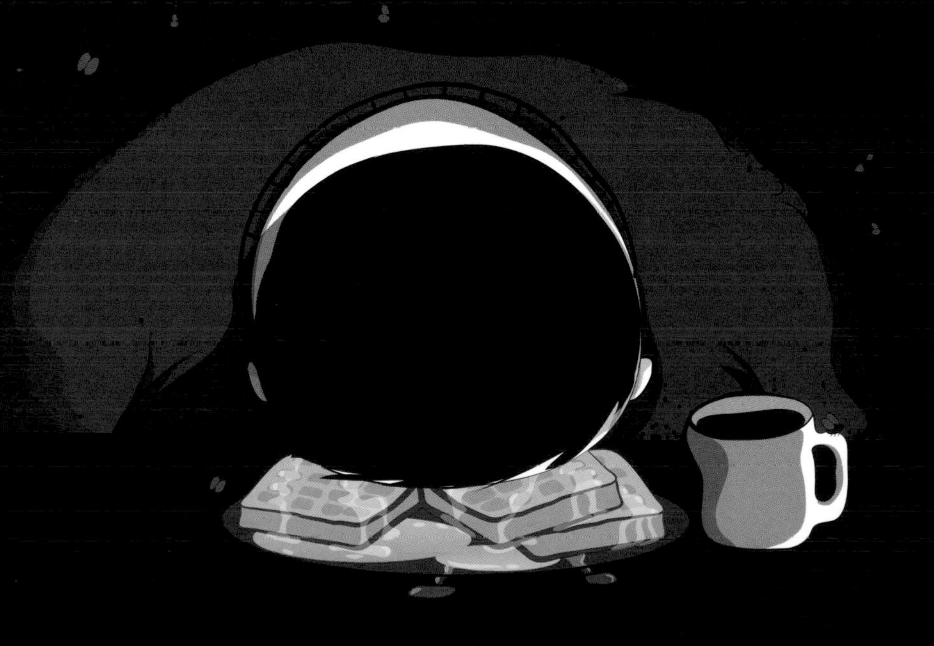

8. Hurt yourself today.

I am neither old nor wise, but I have learned some things.
I've learned that sometimes if I'm having an awesome day,

hurt and awfulness

like to rain down from the sky
and hit me right in my jolly little face.

That's just life.
Sometimes good things happen and
sometimes bad things happen. I'm not in control.

I'm just a jellyfish riding the tormented swells
of a violent, uncaring ocean.

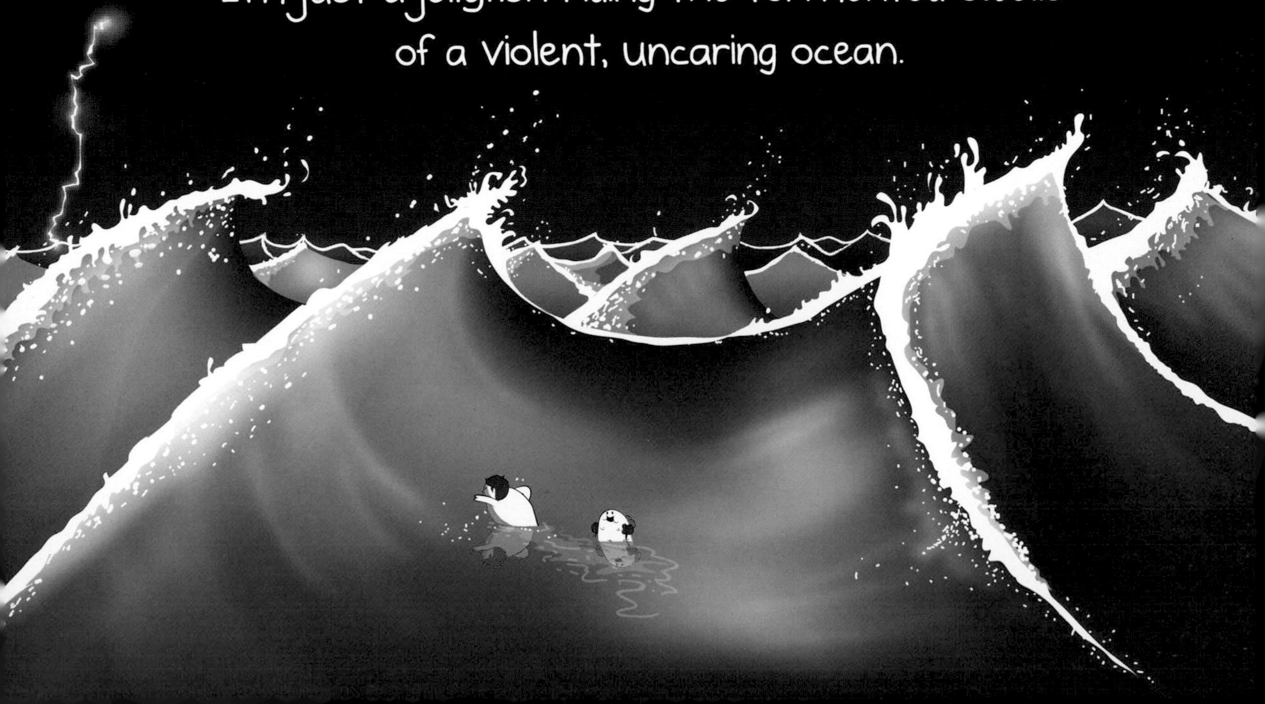

But when I run, *I* control the hurt.

It's a form of hurt I can *possess.*

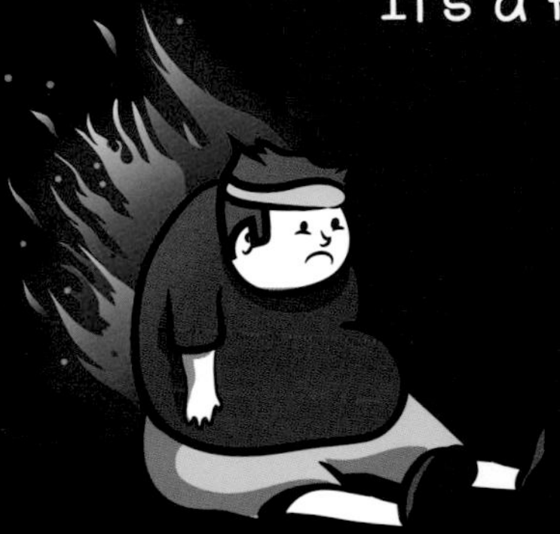

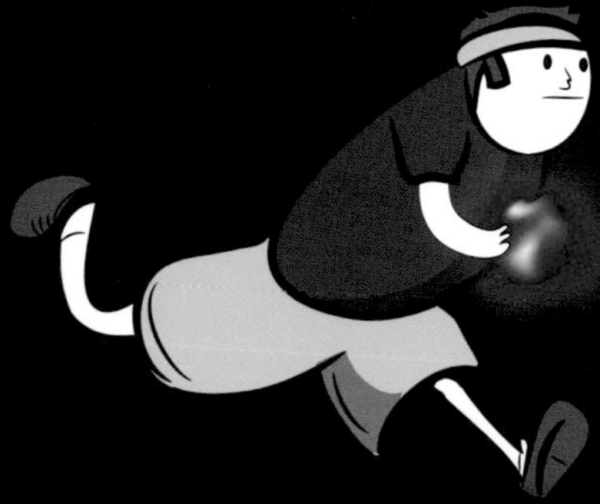

There's an enduring myth that distance runners are impervious to pain — that we're a bunch of freakish stoics who are immune to physical stress. This is not true. Runners aren't impervious to pain, we're just better at *choosing* what kind of pain we have to feel.

And when I run, that's exactly what I'm doing.

I'm asserting control over the uncontrollable.

I'm housebreaking a tornado.

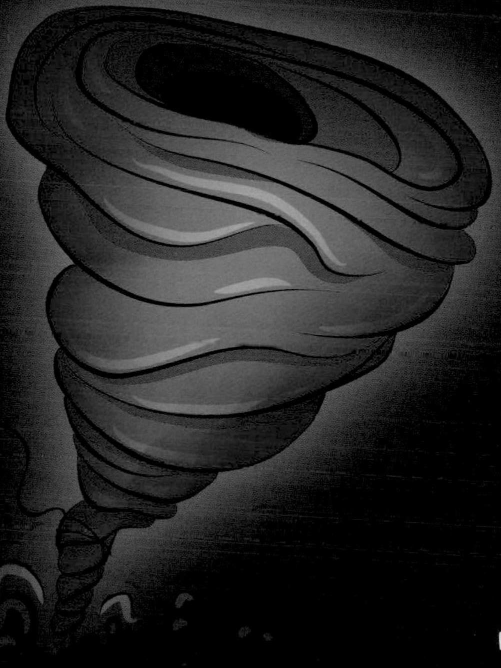

Running is a way of standing up to all the
stupid shit in your life and saying:
*I don't know how to fix you,
so I'll just bend you into workable shapes.*

And the day I put on a pair of running shoes,
I did just that.

I chose *not* to combat my monsters,
I chose to put them on a leash
and take them for a walk instead.

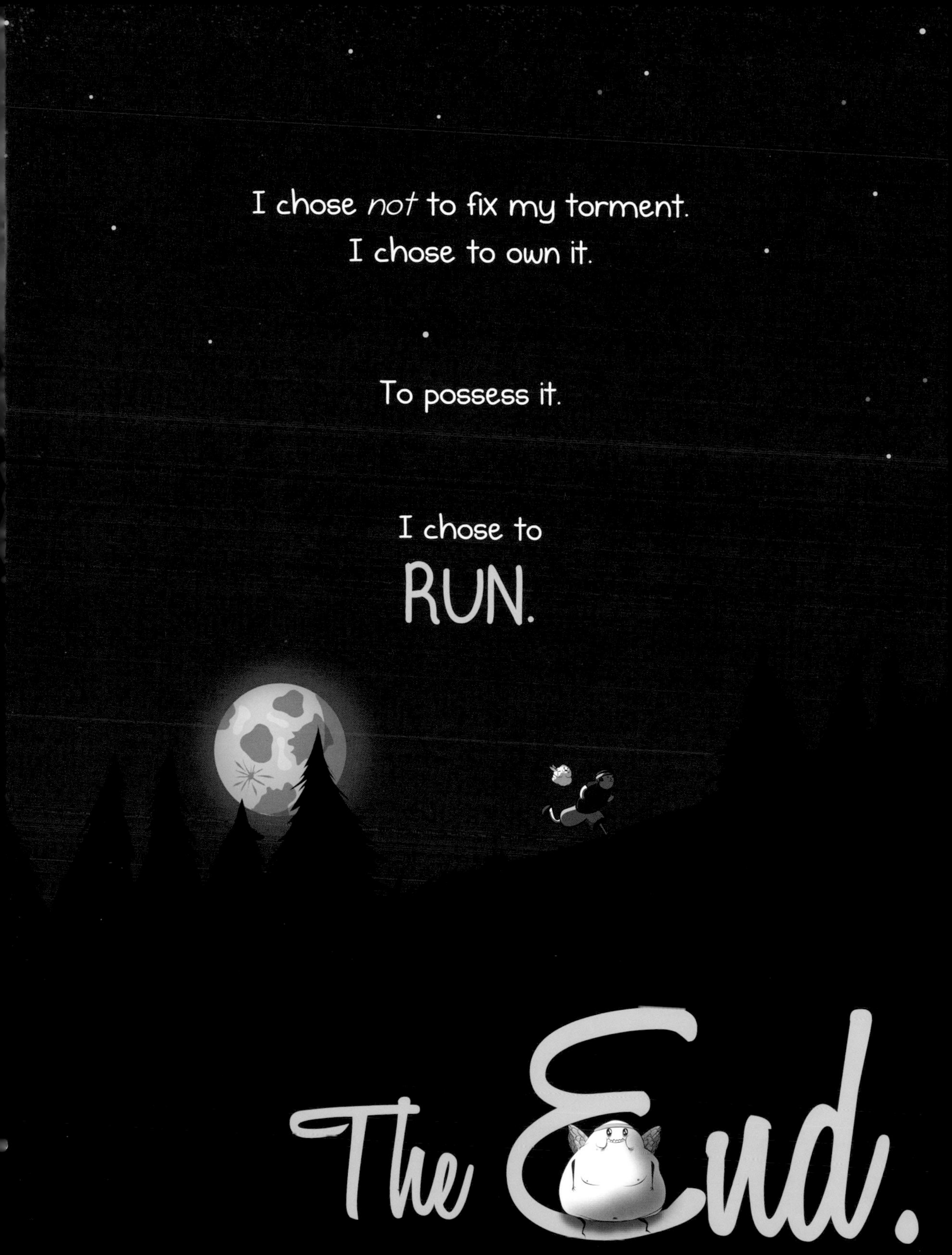

I chose *not* to fix my torment.
I chose to own it.
To possess it.
I chose to
RUN.
The End.

Notes & acknowledgments

The hornet/lightning run:

My crazy bamboo-lightning run happened in the Meitoku neighborhood of Nagoya, Japan, and as far as I know that purple drink is still in those vending machines (although still heavily guarded by winged, nightmare insects).

"I run to seek a void."

This line was paraphrased from *What I Talk About When I Talk About Running*, a wonderful book by Haruki Murakami.

My favorite runs in Seattle:

If I'm looking to just clock some easy miles, I run around Green Lake or on th Burke-Gilman Trail. If I'm looking for hills, I run at Discovery Park. If I'm looking for scenic, well-marked trails, I run at Cougar Mountain. If I'm looking to get stung by nettles and chased by bears, I run at Tiger Mountain. If I'm looking to get accosted by crackheads and pooped on by seagulls, I run downtown.

My favorite distance: Half marathon.

My favorite mid-run snack: Japanese o'nigiri.

My PRs:

I run often but I am by no means an impressive runner. I once ran a half marathon in one hour and thirty minutes, and I can *sometimes* run a sub-six-minute mile, but that's about as competitive as I get.

I am much more competitive when it comes to eating and napping so if these activities are added to the Olympics, please let me know because I will be crowned champ of champs.

About the author

This book was written and drawn by

Matthew Inman,

AKA *The Oatmeal*.

Matthew lives in Seattle, Washington, with his two overweight, poorly behaved dogs, Rambo and Beatrix.

Visit www.theoatmeal.com for more of Matthew's comics, or check out his other books:

→ How to Tell If Your Cat Is Plotting to Kill You

→ My Dog: The Paradox

→ Why Grizzly Bears Should Wear Underpants

→ 5 Very Good Reasons to Punch a Dolphin in the Mouth

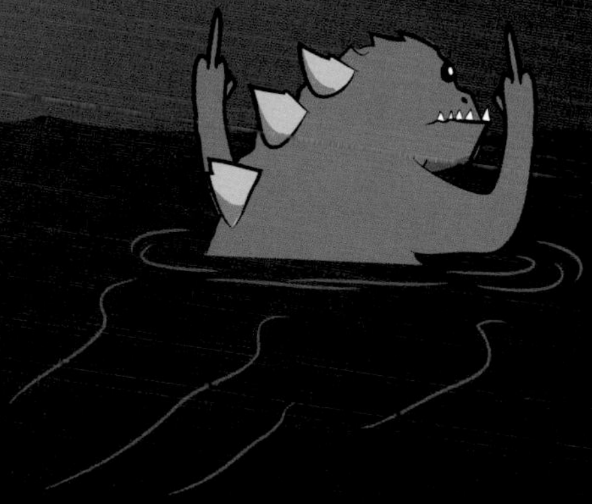

Andrews McMeel Publishing, LLC
an Andrews McMeel Universal company
1130 Walnut Street, Kansas City, Missouri 64106

www.andrewsmcmeel.com

14 15 16 17 18 TEN 10 9 8 7 6 5 4 3 2 1

ISBN: 978-1-4494-5995-6

Library of Congress Control Number: 2014937161

ATTENTION: SCHOOLS AND BUSINESSES
Andrews McMeel books are available at quantity discounts with bulk purchase for educational, business, or sales promotional use. For information, please e-mail the Andrews McMeel Publishing Special Sales Department: specialsales@amuniversal.com.